MW01174256

All Things Guy

A Guide to
Becoming a
Man that Matters

© 2011 Bezalel Books

Published by
Bezalel Books
Waterford, MI

www.BezalelBooks.com

Other great Bezalel Books for young guys:

My Big Feet by Joan L. Kelly
Hiding the Stranger: The Trilogy by Joan L. Kelly
Daily Direction for Teenz by Catherine Wasson-Brown

Printed in the United States of America

All rights reserved. No part of this publication may be reproduced, stored in a retrieval system, or transmitted in any form or by any means—for example, electronic, photocopy, recording—without the prior written permission of the author. The only exception is brief quotations in printed reviews.

Note: References to the Catechism of the Catholic Church are shown as CCC.

Cover images:
Cammeraydave | Dreamstime
Lomachevsky | Dreamstime

ISBN 978-1-936453-06-1

To my precious sons, Jared, Justin, and Jordan, may you always be men that matter and aspire to an eternal life in Heaven. Love, Mom.

To my grand-nephew Eli, welcome to the world. I pray I can help you become a young man of virtue. Love, Aunt Teresa.

Did you ever notice that life seems to have a whole lot of questions? You ask them of yourself, or your parents ask them of you, or your teachers ask, or your friends ask...Yep, life is full of questions. You are being asked questions right now!

Of all the questions ever asked, there's a couple that are really, super important. At first they may not seem like much, but they are actually ultra-important. What are they?

✠ DO YOU WANT TO GROW UP TO BE A HAPPY, SUCCESSFUL MAN?
✠ DO YOU WANT TO MAKE SOMETHING OF YOURSELF ON EARTH, AND THEN, WHEN YOUR LIFE IS OVER, GO TO HEAVEN?

This book is for any guy who answered yes to either of these questions. So, if you've answered yes, at least once, you've got to know what you'll have to do to accomplish either or both goals. You'll have to know important things that may be quite different from whatever you currently think is important. But if you want to become a man that matters, if you really want to spend eternity in Heaven, there are some things that you can do right now to make sure you are on the right track. And if you've never given it much thought, now's the time to do just that.

EITHER WAY, WHATEVER YOUR SITUATION, HERE'S A GUIDE TO BECOMING A MAN THAT MATTERS

Dignity

Ready for a Couple of Big Questions?

1. WHY DID GOD MAKE YOU?
2. WHAT DO YOU NEED TO DO TO GO TO HEAVEN?

Well, first one first...

God created you because He loves you so much that He made you to live with Him in Heaven forever. See, God is the Supreme Being who made all things and He wants to show His goodness and to share with you His everlasting happiness in Heaven; that's why He made you! Yes, you heard right, everlasting happiness! In Heaven, your heart will be so full of the love of God that you will never be unhappy!

There are many stories about God's love for us in the Bible. One of them is the Passion. Jesus loved us so much that he gave his life up on the Cross in order to save us. Wow! This is the greatest love one can express for another!

And to answer the second big question...

To go to Heaven you need to know, love and serve God in this life.

But, how does a guy like you do all that?

By taking it one step at a time:

1. To Know God

It is necessary to find out about God, just like you do when you want to know about your favorite football player. You read about him in the newspaper, magazines, or online. You watch him on TV during the games to see how he plays. With God, you hear about Him from your parents, read about Him in the Bible and in the Catechism of the Catholic Church. At Mass you hear about Him in the readings and the sermon and then in religion classes, too.

2. To Love God

You will love God when you get to know Him because God is Love. When you love someone, you spend time with them. Think of the time you spend with your dad hunting, playing ball, or just hanging out. Or maybe think of the time you spend with a good friend or even one of your cousins. God is all those things and more! So, it makes sense that the same thing goes with God: you spend time thinking about Him and talking with Him in prayer, adoration, and listening to Him speak to you in your heart.

3. To Serve God

Serving God is serving others. This would mean doing your chores without complaining when mom or dad asks you to do them. It's babysitting your little brothers and sisters cheerfully. It's doing homework well. It's being helpful to a cranky neighbor. Anything you do for others you do for God.

Well, that takes a load off, knowing that you have a specific purpose. God is counting on you to make a difference in the world in which you live. But you've gotta ask Him to show you what He wants you to do in your life. This will be your vocation and if you follow it, you will be happy and you will please God.

Man was made in God's image and likeness. No other creature was created in God's image and likeness, so this makes human beings unique. Humans also have free will so they can make all sorts of decisions about their lives. That includes what you want for yourself in the future.

Will you be married, have children, and be a newspaper reporter, or become a priest and do missionary work?

Whatever it is you do, however, you ought to do it with God. When you include God in your life, you are sort of like a satellite dish because you will hear Him and you will be able to communicate with Him much better than if you don't spend time with Him.

There Are Two Dimensions to Man:

✟ THE BODY
✟ THE IMMORTAL SOUL

The body is pretty easy to understand, right? But the soul takes a bit more thought. The soul is what animates the body and this is the part that is "like" God. He is all spirit. This is the part of Man that lives forever. Because of this, Man has a special dignity and is above the animals.

The spiritual tradition of the Church
also emphasizes the *heart* ...
where the person decides for or against God.
CCC# 368

Who's Your Daddy?

Being born male is no coincidence. From all eternity God knew you and made you a boy on purpose. Yep, he picked your parents, what you look like, and he knows what you will be when you grow up. You see, you are very important to God and to His kingdom. Why? Because you are His child! You are a son of God! This is one of the most awesome gifts that you will ever receive!

In your life, you will go through good times and rough times, you will accomplish great things, but perhaps you will also have disappointments; all these are part of life!

You may encounter people who tell you things like:

- You are a loser if you don't get a high paying job, a beautiful huge house, a sports car and money to travel around the world when you get older.
- You are nobody if you don't succeed as a baseball player and get a scholarship.
- You are worth nothing unless you achieve fame and people praise you and think you are amazing.

These are all nonsense! You better not believe them! Always remember that the fact that you are a son of God is what defines you as a person! This is your greatness, your highest dignity!

Being created in the image of God gives you the dignity of a person.

Dignity Has Three Unique Characteristics:

✟ IT IS NOT DEPENDENT ON ANY CIRCUMSTANCES

 WITHIN WHICH YOU LIVE.

✟ IT DOESN'T MATTER WHAT YOU LOOK LIKE.

✟ IT DOES NOT CHANGE, EVEN WHEN YOU DO.

The dignity of the human person is rooted in his creation in the image and likeness of God.
CCC # 1700

- Dan was in the Gulf War and lost both his legs and uses prostheses (fake limbs) to walk.

- Your friend's grandpa is in the nursing home, unable to get out of bed to even go to the bathroom.

- Tim has won two gold medals in the Olympics.

- Rob is African, lives in a hut, and goes to school in Kenya.

- Jim is chubby and has always struggled with being the "fat kid."

- Ben is a skateboarder who everyone thinks is cool.

- Scott loves school and gets great grades, while David is the biggest tattletale and is always getting other kids in trouble.

- Tom's mom and dad are divorced and he lives in government-provided housing.

- Brad's Dad is a doctor and they live in a big house and go on fancy vacations, while Dylan has trouble in school and people think he's dumb.

WHAT'S THE BIG NEWS?

All these guys have *equal dignity.*
They are all equal in worth and value as people.
This is true for *all* people, male and female.
It's important to feel good about yourself as a son of God and to know that is the source of your dignity.

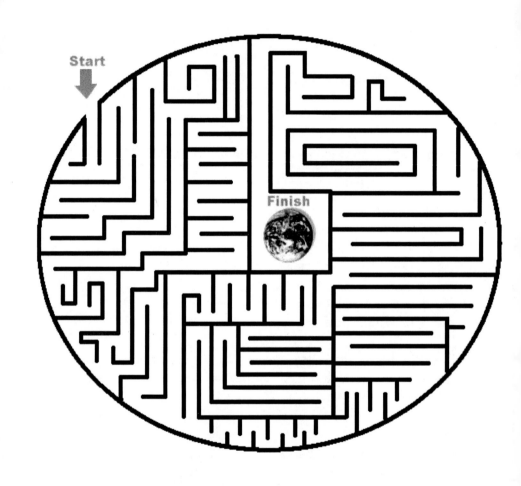

Start

Finish

Virtues and More

Virtues to Live By

Virtues are good habits. They are characteristics that are valued in people. You get 'em by practicing good actions over and over again:

- ✟ Having patience when waiting in line
- ✟ Doing chores without complaining
- ✟ Doing your best on your schoolwork
- ✟ Sharing your things
- ✟ Keeping your mouth shut when you feel like saying something less than nice

> **You get the picture.**
> **Simple, but not easy.**

Do you want to become a man that matters? Of course you do! So here are some of the virtues that will help you.

Courage

One virtue that's important to practice for guys is courage. To be a real man you gotta have courage.

Courage is a virtue worth developing! Courage is the ability to confront fear, pain, risk, danger and uncertainty. You have probably read stories about courageous things that people have done—like firefighters who enter buildings to save others—or how seriously ill people endured their difficulties and trials. You have most definitely heard of athletes who train and give their "all" to their sport.

Whether it be an Olympic medal, surviving an illness, or rescuing someone stranded in a fire, no hardship seemed too difficult for these people to overcome because they were motivated by a goal. They took risks and persevered. They were patient in the face of adversity. They were courageous.

Martyrdom is the greatest act of fortitude and courage. It's giving your life in defense of your faith. However, God does not ask the majority of Christians to shed their blood in testimony of the faith they profess. But He does ask you to be courageous in your ordinary life.

One of the ways to practice courage is by cheerfully accepting some of your daily difficulties, annoyances, hardships, and even sufferings. When you get into the habit of practicing courage in the small things of life, then, when something big comes up, you will be able to face it and endure it with a much better attitude!

Some examples of being courageous in your daily life are:

- ✝ Not complaining or whining when you don't feel good or have a headache
- ✝ Getting up on time and going to bed on time at night
- ✝ Eating what your mom made for supper without complaining, even if it's not your favorite dish
- ✝ Giving up your favorite TV show in order to watch your brother's choice
- ✝ Doing your homework right away instead of playing videogames or sports
- ✝ Saying *no* when your peers ask you to do something you know is wrong

✞ Defending a kid at school who is being picked on by other kids
✞ Offering help to others when you would rather spend time at the computer

Courage is bravery. All the saints and heroes practiced courage. Courage is the virtue of a soldier in the battlefield. If you want to be a Soldier for Christ, practice courage!

Self-Control

Self-control is a virtue of real men. It requires your strength and your toughness. Many people measure strength by how many pounds a person can lift. But true strength is self mastery, the ability to keep yourself under control.

Self-Control is another virtue that is great to have!

It's a virtue that characterizes great leaders! It refers to the ability to control your behavior through the use of your will. It's putting your head in control of what your body demands—especially when the demands include being lazy and reluctant to carry out your responsibilities.

Virtue is a habitual and firm disposition to do good.
CCC# 1833

Here are a few examples
of Self-Control:

✝ Not overindulging in
   food or drink. Are you
   able to eat a couple of
   chocolate-chip cookies and not the whole batch?
✝ Behaving differently in Church than you do on a
   soccer field. Does your behavior show that you
   know the sacredness of God's home?
✝ Finishing a task without making excuses to
   interrupt it. When Mom asks you to vacuum the
   house, do you stop vacuuming to take a break
   every 5 minutes?
✝ Not losing your temper when someone provokes
   you. When your little sister annoys you, do you
   lose your temper and yell at her?
✝ Not interrupting other people's conversation. Do
   you wait for the right time to say what you need
   to say when others are speaking?
✝ Being responsible when you have made a
   commitment. Do you make up an excuse for not
   shoveling your neighbor's driveway because you
   prefer to do something more fun with a friend?
✝ Sticking to a plan of personal hygiene. Do you
   take a shower and brush your teeth every day,
   even if you are tired?
✝ Honoring everyone's dignity. Do you see every
   person as having dignity and deserving respect,
   even when your friends are making fun of
   someone?
✝ Having a time limit to play video games and
   computer. Are you able to turn off your Xbox 360
   after playing for a while and find something else
   to do?

May We Have a Word About Boredom?

Boredom is an emotional state you experience when you don't have anything to do or are not interested in anything everyone else is doing. Boredom is not a good thing; sometimes it can make you miserable. When you go and tell your mom, *"I'm bored, I don't know what to do,"* it's like poking her with a stick in the side. Moms don't like to hear this! If you are feeling bored, it's time to use your self-mastery and get rid of your boredom by making yourself do something productive. It will take effort to start an activity, but soon boredom goes away and you feel much better.

Don't forget to ask for Jesus' help!

And definitely don't plop down on the couch because you are bored. Do something good for you and good for God.

Self-control is a lifelong task! Start today by practicing small ways to be in control of yourself. Remember, people that have self mastery make great bosses, are confident leaders, and people enjoy working with them. And most of all, they are happy people because they are in control of themselves!

The King and I

Guys, being Catholic is a gift. Why? Because no other faith has Jesus in the Eucharist. Anytime you want, you can go and sit close to the King of Kings in any Catholic Church because He is there in the Tabernacle. Knowing this, it's a good idea to dress and act like you are in the presence of the King of Kings.

Here in the U.S., we do not have a royal family. But there are still countries such as Spain and England that have a monarchy. They have special rules of etiquette that must be followed if you are in the presence of the king or queen. The same is true for you, going into a Catholic Church. Maybe you aren't aware of certain rules, so let's go over the basic etiquette to use when you are in a Catholic Church. These apply for a short visit or when at Mass.

Always remove your hat when entering a Church. Genuflect upon entering the church. You make a good genuflection by bending your right knee all the way to the ground and bowing your head. Make the sign of the cross reverently as you rise. This is a way to say "Hi" to Jesus in the Tabernacle. You are showing that you realize He is there.

Dude, don't show up to Mass in your grubby, torn jeans and t-shirt. Remember you are there to see the King. Jesus appreciates your effort when you comb your hair, brush your teeth, and wear dress clothes when you go to Mass.

Even though it's the "style" now for guys to wear their pants low and baggy, pull your pants up to your waist for Mass. You may think you look weird, but in reality you look respectful if you wear your shirt tucked in and your pants at least close to your natural waist. It may be a sacrifice for you, but JUST DO IT! If it seems too difficult, consider the sacrifice Jesus made for you, on the cross, and you'll see that dressing appropriately for Church isn't something to complain about to your parents. Besides, you can offer it up and Jesus will appreciate it and so will those sitting around you. Remember, it's not all about you!

While on the subject of appearance for Mass, guys, wear dress shoes and not your tennis shoes. If you serve Mass, it's especially important that you wear dress shoes. You may not care, but if you are wearing ratty shoes at the altar, it is a distraction for those in the congregation.

Make sure you sit up straight and try to keep your mind on the Mass and what is going on. It's easy to get distracted but continue to bring your mind back to the Sacrifice of Jesus. You may want to concentrate on one of the statues or stained glass windows in your Church. That's why they're there, to help people stay focused on Our Lord.

Spit out your gum before you come to Church. Never, ever chew gum during Mass. It is one of the most disrespectful things ever.

Keep the hour of fast before Holy Communion. This includes not eating, chewing gum, or drinking (except for water.) Keeping the fast is a way to show Jesus that you really care about preparing yourself to receive Him in Holy Communion.

After Communion, take your time and talk with Jesus, not only thanking Him for coming to you, but about things on your mind. He is so close to you that after Communion is the perfect time to bring all your concerns to Him. There's also a cool thing you can do. When you're in line waiting to receive Communion, think of Mary, the Blessed Mother and ask her to come to Communion with you. Then when you get back to your pew, you can give Mary her Son who is now inside you.

The Virgin Mary can help you talk to Jesus about all the things on your mind. If you do this, you have two times the amount of prayers going to Jesus—yours and Mary's. Always remember, Mary is there to help you get to know her Son and to help you get to Heaven. Take advantage of a mom with REAL power, your Blessed Mother.

Now that you know about Jesus in the Tabernacle, it is also a good idea to remove your hat even when you are just passing a Church because He is in there. If you don't have a hat on, make the sign of the cross to recognize His presence.

ANIMA CHRISTI

Soul of Christ, sanctify me.
Body of Christ, save me.
Blood of Christ, inebriate me.
Water from the side of Christ, wash me.
Passion of Christ, strengthen me.
Oh good Jesus, hear me.
Within Thy wounds hide me.
Suffer me not to be separated from Thee.
From the malignant enemy, defend me.
In the hour of my death, call me.
And bid me come to Thee.
That with Thy saints I may praise Thee.

Sportsmanship

Everyone enjoys playing sports with someone who doesn't whine when he loses, or doesn't brag to the whole world when he scores a touchdown. Sportsmanship is the virtue of people who are "good sports." Being a good sport involves being a good winner as well as being a good loser. It also involves not having the attitude of "win at all costs."

Here are some examples of good sportsmanship:

- Playing fair and being honest in the game
- Respecting your team members, opponents, spectators, and referees
- Shaking hands with the opposite team after the game, even if your team lost
- Showing up at practice and working hard to improve your game
- Sharing equipment with teammates and opponents
- Not taking advantage of injured opponents

What about sore losers? People that display poor sportsmanship are often called "Sore Losers." And as bad as sore losers are, obnoxious winners are no better!

Here are some examples of being a sore loser or an obnoxious winner:

- Whining and complaining about everything from the bad ref calls to the sun in your eyes when you are on the team that lost
- Holding grudges when you lose or when you think the game wasn't fair
- "Booing" the winner's national anthem, or the player's names at an event

- Losing your temper when you make a mistake in the game
- Quitting before the end of the match
- "Rubbing salt in the wounds" of the team you just beat; you already won, give 'em a break
- Laughing at another team's players, skills, or uniforms
- Starting or spreading rumors or lies just to make the other guys look bad

Sports are a great way to learn to get along with others, to learn self-control, and to set goals and challenges for yourself so that you can become a man that matters.

Just remember to be a good sport!

Responsibility

Responsibility is a virtue that helps you follow through on your duties and obligations. If you are responsible, you are reliable; that means that you do as you promised, people can count on you! People don't want to deal with those who are unreliable or blame others for their mistakes.

Responsibility is a virtue that you can develop as you become a man that matters!

You can be sure that most people would rather deal with someone whom they can count on. People who are irresponsible often go against the rules and are not trustworthy. This may sometimes seem like a perfectly okay thing when a boy is young but it will only be a bad thing as he becomes a man that matters.

Responsible people...

☩ **Accept the consequences of their actions:** If you choose not to study for a test, you know the consequence will be a bad grade and you accept that it is your fault.

☩ **Serve others instead of "serving their own preferences":** At dinnertime, you make sure others have a drink before you get your own.

☩ **Do what they have to do – their duties – even if they don't feel like it:** Your Saturday morning chore is to clean the bathroom; you do it without having to be persuaded, even if you would rather do other things. You finish the job without needing your dad to be next to you, making sure the job gets done and you don't goof around.

☩ **Don't make up excuses or blame others for their mistakes:** You don't blame your teacher for a bad grade in math, when it's obvious it was your mistake solving the problems.

☩ **Realize that if they neglect their duty, they are affecting others:** When working on a school project with a few of your classmates, you do your part of the project because you know that if you don't, it will affect everybody's grade on your team.

☩ **Stick to a commitment until finished, whether it is sports, music lessons, clubs, etc.:** If you signed up for band at school, but after a couple of months you found it boring, you stick to it till the end of the semester.

☩ **Use their allowance and earned money for useful things:** When you get paid for a job, you set some money aside to give to your Church or a charity; then you decide if you really need to spend the rest, or if you can put it into your savings.

✟ **Replace things when they damage them:** If you broke your mom's lamp when you were wrestling with your little brother, you try to fix it and if it can't be fixed, you offer to pay for a new one.

A responsible person has great character!

Patriotism

Patriotism is the virtue of love and devotion to one's country. It's recognizing what your country has given you, such as economic opportunities, protection, and a system of law and order. Patriotism is understanding that you don't just take from your country; you give to it, as well.

Some examples of patriotism that you can practice:

✟ Keep your country clean
✟ Celebrate national holidays—don't just look at national holidays as a day off of school
✟ Recite the Pledge of Allegiance with respect and your hand placed upon your heart— remove any hat you may be wearing
✟ Honor your country's flag
✟ Show interest in the history of your country

When you become an adult...

- ✞ Take an active role by doing research before voting.
- ✞ Work to support good candidates.
- ✞ Serve your country in the military.
- ✞ Volunteer to help around the country where natural disasters like floods, earthquakes, or tornadoes have occurred.
- ✞ Obey the laws.
- ✞ Respect authority.

Along with patriotism, there is citizenship. You are a citizen of a country. This is what makes you American, Mexican, or French for example. There are a lot of rights and responsibilities that come with citizenship in a country. In many instances, people have died to help obtain the rights and freedoms everyone enjoys.

This is why gratitude to those who are in your history—and obviously knowing about them—is important. Just like there are Catholics who have gone before you in your faith history, so there are county-men who have gone before you in your nation's history.

However, first and foremost your citizenship is in Heaven. You have a place there because you were baptized. This is your calling—your destiny. Granted, you're not there yet. You have some work to do in order to get there. It began with your baptism and continues each day that you do your best to live for Jesus. Always remember that you have to know, love and serve God before you can become a citizen of Heaven for good! But you can do it if you persevere in this life on earth.

Think about it: in order to be a good citizen here on earth you have responsibilities. As you grow up and become a man, it's important that you learn about your country and what goes on in it. That'll be part history and part current events. You need to know what happened before—so mistakes don't have to be made over and over again—and what's happening now.

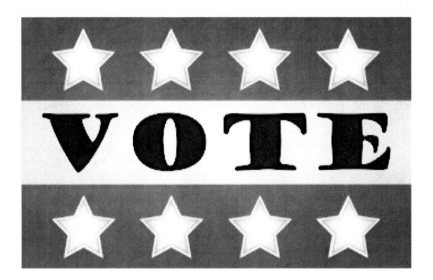

When you turn 18, you can register to vote. This is an honor and a privilege. Make sure you are informed when you go to use this privilege. Use your citizenship on earth as a way to see how important your citizenship is in Heaven!

Being a good citizen allows you to practice great traits, develop a virtuous attitude, and show others that you are interested in becoming a man that matters. You will get to vote, and your vote—along with many others— will be responsible for the things that happen in government. You will want to be an informed voter to be a good citizen; but remember that there are many different ways to inform yourself and studying Church teachings should always be at the top of the list. The Church teaches that you should be a good citizen of your country. The Church knows that God put you where you are today because you matter! Whatever you do with your life, when you answer God's call for your vocation, it is part of God's plan.

It is the duty of citizens to contribute along with the civil authorities to the good of society in a spirit of truth, justice, solidarity, and freedom.
CCC# 2239

Media
and
Men that Matter

Your Future Is Here

Would you like to go to college someday? Are you interested in becoming a priest, a doctor, an engineer, or a world class chef? And although marriage and family are far off in your future, it's probably not a stretch to say that someday you would like to have children of your own. You have these goals because God put them in your heart and whether we realize it or not, we are all called to a special vocation and a life that matters. We are all called to make a difference and in our own unique way to help grow God's Kingdom on earth.

You might be wondering what your answers to any of the big life questions have to do with the media. Well, when you stop and think about it, they have a lot to do with the media, especially when it comes to you growing into a man of virtue, a man that's going to make his special mark on the world.

Don't get me wrong. You already matter—big time—in God's eyes; every person on the planet—boy or girl, big or small—matters to God. You don't have to do a thing to be on God's radar screen. The Lord loves you right where you're at and you don't have to go to college or *do* anything out-of-the-world-extraordinary for God to go on loving you.

Think about the people in your life that you love; your parents, your brothers and sisters, your grandparents and many others. If you ask them they will also tell you what God tells you; that they love you no matter what. That said, when you really love someone you want to show them that love by loving them back and doing nice things for them. You don't have to; but it is a natural reaction and it emulates God's love for people as well as the way people love God.

Jesus tells us in the Gospel of St. John Chapter 10:10 that in addition to loving us, He has great plans for us to live what He calls "the abundant life." How's that for a sweet deal? The Creator of the universe, our Heavenly Father, loves us more than even our earthly dads and on top of that, He wants to make sure we make the most of this life before going to be with Him in the next. He also loves us so much that He even gives us really cool instructions to follow that will help us be who we are called to be and have a happy and fulfilled life. If we truly love Jesus, we will want to follow His plan and do for Him as we would for others we love so dearly.

It all starts with the Bible, which I like to say is an acronym for "**B**asic **I**nstructions **B**efore **L**eaving **E**arth." Get it? Clever, huh? Father does indeed know best and the Bible, which is God's inspired word, guides us along the way. In addition to those basic instructions, as Catholics we have an endless supply of great role models in the lives of saints and teachings in the *Catechism of the Catholic Church* and other writings that can help keep us focused and faithful.

And that's where the media come in. Too much of the media can mean too much noise in our lives—noise that silences the saints and the signals God is trying to send us. Pope Benedict XVI tells us this about noise from our world..."*simply put, we are no longer able to hear God. There are too many frequencies filling our ears.*"

Let's take a look at how the many media frequencies might interfere or cause problems with your big plans for the future as well as your plans to grow up to be a man that would make both your earthly father and your Heavenly Father proud.

Let's start with some questions you might want to ask yourself and discuss with your parents:

- How much time do I spend watching TV, on the computer, on the phone, or listening to music?
- Do my media choices in any way go against the Church and the Bible?
- Do my media choices, such as a website or video, contain too much violence, or content that degrades my family's values?
- Do my media choices promote un-Godly ideas that could lead me away from God and the Church?
- Do my media choices mock parental authority or degrade girls or women in any way?
- Am I using a media outlet such as a cell phone or the Internet to insult, bully, or talk about someone behind their backs?
- Do my media habits interfere with prayer time, Mass, and family time—especially meal-time?

Keep these questions in the back of your mind as we walk through how the media can impact your life now and in the future.

Think B4 U Send!

If you're like most young people today, you spend about the same time using various sorts of media, including a computer, TV, cell phone, or i-pod, as most people do on a full-time job every week. That's right. On average most children and teens spend close to 40 hours a week with some form of media.

While the Internet, cell phones, and other electronic devices can be great tools to help us learn more about our faith, our world, and to keep in touch with family and friends, they can also lead to problems if we're not careful.

The Internet, for example, can send a written message, a video clip, or a photo off into cyber space in a split second. And while you meant the information to be seen by a handful of close companions, it's **NBD** for someone half way across the country to be reading *your* message or looking at *your* picture. You might be thinking **NP.** Well, think again. Did you know that many colleges and universities now regularly check out applicants' profiles on popular social networking sites?

According to the latest research one out of 10 admissions officers looked at applicants' sites as part of their evaluations. One survey of approximately 320 college officials also showed that nearly 40 percent said that seeing questionable material on an applicant's page or profile had a negative impact on the school acceptance decision. Others say they conduct simple searches of e-mail addresses to see what applicants might be up to. So how you communicate and express yourself **DOES** say a lot about you and if you are using the Internet in a questionable way, it could catch up with you and impact you for a very long time.

But the media and its connection to becoming a man of virtue goes even deeper than whether your future plans for a higher education—and ultimately a career—might be affected. Acting in an inappropriate way, whether it's over the Internet, on the cell phone, or in person, is not cool for a Godly guy.

Go to the Bible and check out the verse that's commonly known as "The Golden Rule." You'll find it in the 7th Chapter of St. Matthew's Gospel and here's what it says:

> *In everything, treat people the same way you want them to treat you, for this is the law of the prophets.*

Jesus is telling us that we need to stop and think before we act. We need to think about how we would feel if someone committed a mean, selfish or inconsiderate act against us. How would you feel if one of your classmates or neighborhood buddies embarrassed you—or maybe a friend, sister, or brother? It's not fun to be taunted, teased, or insulted. And having your college plans postponed or nixed because of the click of a button is certainly no fun, not cool, and not the sign of a young man that matters: **So think B4 U Send!**

Life is the Real Deal

As we just pointed out, sometimes it is easy to get sidetracked or led in the wrong direction by the media. TV, the movies, music videos, and violent video games are a big part of most young people's world, but that world can quickly get distorted. The reality is that it can even get dangerous if you start to believe all the messages being beamed at you 24/7. And in many real-life cases, the media influence impacts a young person so much that it isn't only college plans that get ruined. Things that come after college, like career and family, are also affected. Any type of "future" can be wiped out, or drastically changed, if a young man isn't smart and aware of how the media—and that means all your video games, movies, Internet, etc.—operates.

Take the case of a young man in Florida, several years ago. This 14 year old enjoyed watching professional wrestling on TV. It's cool, right? He also liked imitating the moves he saw on the wrestling matches. One fateful afternoon he was playing in his room with a younger friend. He told his mom he didn't mean to hurt the friend; he was just trying to copy some of the slick wrestling moves he watched on TV. He thought his friend would get up from the floor and start playing with him all over again. After all, that's what happened with the professional wrestlers on television every week. But that's not what happened in this real life story. His friend died and the 14 year old was sentenced to life in prison! This young man couldn't distinguish between fact and fiction or reality and fantasy. To him, TV was real. He didn't understand that professional wrestling is staged or acted out and that in real life you can get hurt.

You think you're smarter than that, though, right? And maybe you are in this one instance, but consider that there may be other ways where you aren't as smart as you should be. We never always know what our weaknesses really are and so we always ought to be on guard against things that take our minds or thoughts in directions that are different than what our family teaches or negatively affects how we live.

There are many other sad cases of middle school or high school students who also acted out what they saw in a violent movie, video game, or on a TV crime program. We've seen the result of this in school shootings, on school playgrounds, or at the mall. Did you know that if you continue to consume the level of 40 hours of media a week, that by the time you reach 13 you will have witnessed 100 thousand violent acts on TV? That number will double by the time you reach high school graduation. Viewing repeated acts of violence desensitizes a person which means that you could start thinking that violence is a normal way to react to a situation. But Jesus tells us in the Gospel of St. Luke 22:38 that violence is never the answer and that "those who live by the sword, die by the sword."

Dads Deserve Better

Ever notice how dads are portrayed in the media, especially in television shows? Usually they are not shown as the kind, loving husband who is also a strong, capable leader. Instead, today's TV dads are mostly portrayed as the flustered and useless member of the household who couldn't help with the family responsibilities if his life depended on it. If a dad is shown in a good light in a TV sitcom or movie, then it's only because the mom character has whipped him into shape or he was forced to learn how to fend for himself and family because the mom is no longer part of the plot.

I don't know about you, but that's not a fair picture of my dad and it probably doesn't represent your dad fairly, either. But here's the deal, guys, remember our earlier point about how media desensitizes us? Well, if you keep watching shows that insult fatherhood, how is it going to make you feel about a) your dad, b) our Heavenly Father, and c) how are you going to feel about getting married and raising a family when you grow up?

So how about backing away from the TV, putting down the remote for a while, and picking up the Bible instead? The Bible is full of real heroes; real men that made a difference and knew what mattered: Moses, Daniel, King David, St. Joseph, St. Peter, and St. Paul. The list is endless and that list only includes a small number of those we now honor in the Catholic faith.

Moses challenged the great Egyptian leaders to free the Jewish people from captivity. Daniel had the gift of prophecy and his dedication to God got him thrown in the lions' den but he walked out without a scratch! David fought the giant Goliath and won and went on to lead the Jewish people, with Almighty God eventually referring to him as *a man after my own heart.* St. Joseph, Jesus' foster father or earthly guardian, protected and loved our Lord and our Blessed Mother, even when it put him, his work, and his reputation in danger. St. Peter became the first Pope and when he was crucified in Rome, he insisted that he be crucified upside down because he felt he wasn't worthy to die in the same manner on the cross as our Lord. St. Paul, the great evangelist, was stoned, whipped, beaten, shipwrecked, imprisoned, and that's just for starters.

All of these men, despite the countless obstacles and persecution they faced, went on to do great things for God and for the entire Christian world. But these warriors for the faith knew first and foremost that at the end of the day, all that mattered was their relationship with God and whether they honored that relationship by doing what they could to evangelize and spread His Kingdom. These men were not wimps – they were warriors for the Lord. While they may have lived at different times in history, they had many things in common. In addition to their love for God, they were keenly aware of how worldly influences could pull someone away from their faith. And while they didn't have radio, TV, or the Internet, they knew that there were plenty of temptations out there that could lead to spiritual confusion and moral decay. St. Paul addresses this directly in Chapter 4 of his *Letter to the Ephesians*:

> *Then we will no longer be infants, tossed back and forth by the waves, and blown here and there by every wind of teaching and by the cunning and craftiness of men in their deceitful scheming.*
>
> *Instead, speaking the truth in love, we will in all things grow up into him who is the Head, that is, Christ. From him the whole body, joined and held together by every supporting ligament, grows and builds itself up in love, as each part does its work.*

So, do you want to be pulled in every different direction, tossed around emotionally and spiritually by something you see on television or in a video game? Or do you want to be a young man of virtue? It's your choice.

What Would Jesus Do?

A few years ago there was a really popular wrist band that lots of young people were wearing. The wristbands came in different colors but had the same letters printed on them: WWJD. Those letters represented a question: What would Jesus do?

W.W.J.D.?

The wristbands were a reminder for Christian teens to put Christ first in everything, especially when it came to the choices they made. If they were feeling peer pressure to do something that was wrong, the bracelet provided a gentle reminder to ask themselves that question. When you think about what Jesus would do, it's much easier for you to do the right thing.

Now let's take that idea one step further. Imagine yourself sitting in front of the computer or TV and seeing a commercial or a music video that makes girls or women seem like objects by the way they are dressed or the way they are acting with, or around, boys. Maybe you are on a popular social site and someone is sending around pictures that may harm a person's reputation. What would Jesus do and how would you feel if you were watching that clip with Jesus sitting right beside you? If it makes you feel uncomfortable or embarrassed, well, that's the Holy Spirit letting you know that it is time to change channels or back away from the computer. That is, after all, what Jesus would do. Jesus would never support anything that would insult or impact our dignity as human beings. Jesus, as a matter of fact, was *the* greatest liberator of all human beings and He wanted it to be abundantly clear that women had great dignity. And, in any of these scenarios, you should also be aware that sometimes the least popular but most "right" answer is to tell an adult about what is going on.

Do you know 2000 years ago when Jesus walked the earth, women were considered property? They could not even serve as a witness in court because their testimony was not considered worthy or valid. Yet what did Jesus do? He changed all of that and treated women as equals, made them part of His ministry. He knew that people needed to understand that God loved women as much as God loved men.

Jesus talked with women one on one, and gave them some of the greatest privileges when it came to evangelization. God hand-picked the Blessed Mother to bring Jesus into the world through the Incarnation, or the "Word Becoming Flesh." And He also chose St. Mary Magdalene to be the first to encounter Him after the resurrection!

The Catholic Church continues this tradition of honoring women. Mary, the Blessed Mother, has been given many beautiful titles including "Queen of Heaven" and our "Universal Mother." Many women in Jesus' day, and over the past two thousand years, have been canonized as saints, and three women saints, St. Teresa of Avila, St. Catherine of Sienna and St. Therese of Lisieux, were named "Doctors" of the Church, a title that honors their influence on the faith and the faithful.

So here's the deal: if Jesus liberates women, honors them, and does everything He can through His Church to uphold and defend their dignity, shouldn't you? Imagine that one of the girls who are being treated poorly will one day be someone's wife; she may one day be your wife! Wouldn't you want to have done all you could to protect her for that person or for yourself?

Sadly, the culture we live in certainly doesn't think so and there is a lot of research to prove that. Recently the American Psychological Association issued a shocking report showing how all forms of media contribute to the disrespect of women. The APA said that women— and girls your age—were made to feel like objects. Why? Because the media—through magazines, movies, and TV commercials and programs—puts too much emphasis on the way a girl looks, what she wears, and how much she weighs. There is simply way too much pressure for girls to grow up way too fast. You don't want to contribute to that, do you?

The peer pressure and the cultural influences are so strong that the APA says they often lead to eating disorders, depression, and other problems. So you need to do what Jesus would do: say "No way!" to those influences that objectify women. You need to treat the ladies in your life as He would, with respect and dignity.

Doing What the World Says vs. Doing What Jesus Says

You now have a pretty good idea that Jesus spoke with both powerful words and powerful acts of love. If you're a Godly guy, you probably also have a good idea of how Jesus would respond in difficult situations. Keep the *"what would Jesus do question"* always in front of you, when temptations come along.

Here are a few final thoughts regarding our discussion of "The Media and Becoming a Man that Matters."

These points will help you avoid being influenced by something you might see or hear in today's media saturated culture.

- By doing what the world says—such as reacting aggressively or in a violent matter—you risk your safety and your future.
- By doing what Jesus says you learn to respond calmly and with love leading to peace in your family and the world.
- By doing what the world says and giving into temptations such as drinking, drugs, or inappropriate relationships, you become susceptible to addictions, sexually transmitted diseases, and other problems too numerous to tell.
- By doing what Jesus says and saying *"no"* to things that degrade people, you live a happy, healthier, and more peaceful life.

Jesus should always be your guide, your best friend, and the one who you are most interested in pleasing. It may not be easy but it is always right.

To become a man that matters, to be a great warrior for Christ, you will always be faced with decisions.

Decide Christ!

Story of Blessed Miguel Pro

"It was really a close call," Miguel was saying to his friends at the hideout. They were listening intently because they could not believe how lucky Miguel was to have narrowly escaped being caught.

"Aren't you afraid?" Jose asked.

Miguel seemed to think about it for a moment and then responded, "No, I am not afraid. It is not right that we cannot practice our Catholic faith in our beautiful Mexico City."

Remembering the recent near-capture of his friend, Jose persisted, "Do you know what will happen to you if you get caught giving communion to our brothers-and-sisters-in-Christ? Or what the authorities will do to you if they see you are providing clothes to the homeless?"

Miguel sighed because he did know what would happen, but Miguel also knew that Christ had a purpose for Miguel's return to Mexico. Miguel knew that he would continue to rely on different disguises so that he could serve others. In some ways, putting on his disguises made him feel young and carefree because they reminded him of his days as a young boy when he would play with his friends. Just days ago he had made his way into the streets dressed as a mechanic. Miguel knew that the authorities were on to him and prayed that the disguises would continue to give him enough cover so that he could accomplish his mission. He so loved being back home.

It had been a few years since he had been sent away from Mexico because of the revolution. He had travelled to such faraway lands as Belgium and Nicaragua and even though he felt privileged to help Catholics in these wonderful places, Miguel knew his heart would always be in Mexico.

Looking Jose straight in the eye, Miguel said, "Jose, I accepted my poor health and my exile because I knew these things came from God. I now accept His mission for my life to take care of others—spiritually and temporally—and when my mission is complete, I trust Jesus will take me home."

That night Miguel went to sleep dreaming of his young childhood days. Miguel had always been a prankster, his mother said, God bless her soul. "High spirited" is what she would say. Miguel knew that was a nice way to say he always had his mother worried. It wasn't that Miguel was a bad kid, just an active one.

"Miguel! I pray to God almighty that you will behave yourself and spend time on your studies!" she had said in her harshest voice after Miguel broke a vase because he was using it as a target for his finely honed slingshot skills.

"I know, Madre, I know! But who could have thought I would be such a good shot?!"

Miguel listened as his mother retreated to her chair where she picked up the rosary and prayed. Miguel knew they were prayers for him and it wasn't until he was much older that he realized or appreciated how important those prayers were in his life.

Miguel's sweet dreams continued until there was a thunderous knocking on the door.

"Is Miguel Pro in this hovel?" the deep voice demanded.

Within seconds, Miguel was being dragged from his bed and placed under arrest. He was being accused of a bombing attempt on the president-elect. Miguel was hated by the revolutionaries because of his work as a priest, taking care of Christ's people.

Jose's words came flooding back to Miguel, who knew his mission for Christ was now complete. Soon he would be facing the firing squad.

When asked if he wanted a blindfold, Miguel refused. Miguel died with his arms outstretched like Jesus on the cross and his lips proclaiming, "Long Live Christ the King!"

Father Pro was born in 1891 and died in 1927

CHRIST THE KING, BY THE INTERCESSION OF BLESSED MIGUEL PRO, I BEG YOU TO ANSWER MY PRAYERS. GIVE ME THE GRACE AND THE STRENGTH NECESSARY TO FOLLOW HIS HEROIC EXAMPLE AND TO LIVE MY CATHOLIC FAITH IN SPITE OF ALL TEMPTATIONS AND ADVERSITIES. AMEN.

A Lesson In Stealing and Greed

One day Marvin was at the store with some friends. Walking around, the sight of watches at the jewelry counter caught their attention. Marvin realized that no one was watching the counter and the shiny watches were so tempting that Marvin quickly put one in his pocket. He didn't even let his friends know but quietly joined them and continued walking around the store.

Within minutes a large man put his hand on Marvin's shoulder. "Son, I am with store security. Please come with me."

Marvin felt sick to his stomach as he followed the security guard to the back of the store where the security offices were located. Marvin's friends watched in dismay as their friend was hauled off.

In the office, Marvin was told that the store could press charges but that they wouldn't. They called Marvin's parents who then came and picked him up. Marvin's parents were told that Marvin was not allowed back into the store—ever!

Marvin's mom and dad were ashamed that Marvin had given in to temptation but knew that his fear and humiliation were almost enough in terms of punishment. Marvin was taken to Confession that weekend and has never set foot back in that store. More than anything, Marvin is grateful that he was caught because now, as an adult, he realizes that he could have grown to do worse things had he not learned his lesson at an early age.

THE TENTH COMMANDMENT FORBIDS GREED AND THE DESIRE TO AMASS EARTHLY GOODS WITHOUT LIMIT. CCC# 2536

Vocations

Dude! Whatcha gonna do with your life?

Have you ever been in a religion class or in Church and Father asks you to think about a vocation? Do you get the feeling you want to crawl in a hole and disappear, fearing he will ask you to become a priest?

A vocation is a call from God. It's not merely a career choice. Everyone, everyone, everyone has a calling from God! The word vocation refers to three different things:

1. Vocation comes with baptism. It's a call to know, love and serve God in your life.
2. Vocation also means, "state in life," such as priesthood, religious life, marriage or single life.
3. Vocation also means a personal relationship you have with Jesus. It's you, yourself, trying to know, love, and serve God.

A Word about Discernment

A vocation is much more than choosing a career or planning your life. You have to discern what God's plans are for you. To discern means that you pray and ask God to show you what he wants for you. Pope John Paul II explained in a paper he wrote called "On the Vocation of the Lay Faithful," that it is a "gradual process, one that happens day by day." So don't look for the answer to fall from the sky. It happens day by day through discernment.

When people choose a career such as becoming a doctor, engineer, fireman, or police officer, they ask themselves questions like:

- What will make me happy?
- How will I make money for myself?

When a person discerns a vocation, he asks himself bigger questions like:

- ✞ **What does God want me to do?**
- ✞ **What will please God most?**
- ✞ **What gifts did God give me to use in life?**

See the difference? The focus in discerning is God, not "me." But the cool thing is, what God wants for you is what will make you happy!

"I" "ME" "GOD"
IT *DOES* MAKES A DIFFERENCE WHICH ONE YOU USE!

Just as Blessed Miguel Pro and our fictional friend, Henri Mailliard—whose story you will read about later—had a specific purpose in life, so do you. It is actually very exciting.

As we mentioned before, there are several vocations, that is, "states in life" for men:

- ✞ **Priesthood and Permanent Deaconate**
- ✞ **Religious Life**
- ✞ **Marriage**
- ✞ **Single Life**

Whichever God calls you to will have its joys, sorrows, and challenges, but you will have peace and joy by using your gifts the way God intended. God loves you very much and will give you all the graces you need to answer his call.

> ## Start asking Jesus, today, to begin helping you see your vocation.

Priesthood

The mission that Christ entrusted to his apostles continues to be exercised in the Church until the end of time through the Sacrament of Holy Orders. Through this Sacrament, men receive the power and grace to perform the sacred duties of bishops, priests, and deacons. Jesus instituted this Sacrament at the Last Supper when He said: "Do this in remembrance of me."

What are the main powers of a priest?

- To celebrate Mass
- To change bread and wine into the body and blood of Christ at Mass
- To forgive sins in the Sacrament of Reconciliation
- To administer the Sacraments

What are the main duties of a priest?

- To live in celibacy; that means, not to get married
- To recite the Divine Office every day. The Divine Office is a series of prayers including

psalms, hymns, scripture and writings on the life of the saints. These prayers come in a book called the Breviary. It takes about an hour every day to recite these prayers
- To assist the dying at any hour of the day or night
- To instruct the people and guard them from harm

The Sacrament of Holy Orders includes three degrees:

1. Deaconate, which refers to Deacons.
2. Presbyterate, which refers to priests.
3. Episcopate, also called High Priesthood, is the fullness of the Sacrament of Holy Orders. It refers to Bishops.

Some beginning signs that a young man may be called to the priesthood are:

☩ He is in the habit of living in a state of grace. This is something all Christians should be doing anyway!
☩ He has a desire to save his soul and the souls of others
☩ He lives the virtues—has a life of good habits
☩ He loves to serve at Mass
☩ He helps others to be good Catholics
☩ He goes to confession often

Priests do not get struck by lightning as their sign from God to become a priest. No, they come to the knowledge of their vocation by reason and grace. As Pope John Paul II indicated, it's a day-by-day thing. Once a young man discerns a vocation to the priesthood, he is educated in a school called a seminary where he and other men will study to become priests.

There are two classes of priests:

1. Diocesan priests: are generally in charge of parishes.
2. Religious priests: are members of a religious order or congregation. They take the vows of poverty, obedience, and chastity and live in community in their order.

Priesthood is the highest dignity on earth because a priest is the representative of Christ on earth! You should always greet a priest with respect. In the olden days, it was proper to kiss the hands of a priest because he brings the people the true and real Jesus in Holy Communion. If you get the opportunity to meet a bishop you would kiss his ring as a sign of respect. You would call him "Excellency."

If you discern that God may be calling you to the priesthood, talk with your parents and your parish priest. They will help and guide you in responding to God's call!

The priests are appointed to act on behalf of men in relation to God, to offer gifts and sacrifices for sins.
CCC# 1539

Permanent Deaconate

Some men are not called to the priesthood but do have a vocation to be in ministry. They can do this by being permanent deacons. After Vatican II, men were able to be ordained as deacons that do not go on to the priesthood. The bishop ordains the man by the laying on of hands.

The deacon assists the bishop and priests at Mass by distributing Holy Communion, proclaiming the Gospel, and preaching. Deacons can administer the Sacrament of Baptism, serve as the Church's witness at the sacrament of Holy Matrimony, and preside at funerals. They cannot hear confession and give absolution, consecrate the bread and wine into the Body and Blood of Christ, anoint the sick, or say Mass.

Religious Life

If you are called to religious life, it means you will not marry but will become part of a religious order. A religious order is a group of men or women that live together in community and dedicate their life to God by following specific devotions set by their founder and working to support their community. There are different steps in order to be admitted into a religious order. It's all a process to help the candidate discern his vocation, and once he wishes to be permanently admitted he is required to take the vows of poverty, chastity, and obedience.

Monk, Friar, Brother, what's the difference?

- <u>Monks</u> are male members of religious orders who take vows and live a cloistered or enclosed life, within their monastery. This means that they are separated from the affairs of the external world. Monks pray the Divine Office together every day and live a self-sufficient life. Examples of these religious orders are the Cistercian Monks, who follow the Rule of St. Benedict, and the Carthusian Monks, founded by St. Bruno.

- <u>Friars or Brothers</u> are men consecrated to religious life whose order requires them to live the vows of poverty, chastity, and obedience by serving the community as teachers, doctors, nurses, etc. Friars are supported by donations or charity. Examples of these religious orders are the Franciscans and the Benedictines.

There are four main religious orders:

1. Carmelites: Founded in 1155 on Mount Carmel
2. Franciscans: founded in 1209 by St. Francis of Assisi
3. Dominicans: founded in 1216 by St. Dominic
4. Augustinians: founded in 1255, following the Rule of St. Augustine

There are many more religious orders; some of them derive from one of the above. Some examples are: Capuchins, Benedictines, Salesians, Third Order of St. Francis, etc.

Mrs. Jones invited Father Martin to dinner. She wanted Father to help her teach her young sons about God. Mrs. Jones wanted her boys to see that God was everywhere and in every person.

Dinner was wonderful and 7 year old Luke asked to be excused before dessert. Mr. Jones excused Luke from the table. With only Matthew staying for dessert, Father decided he had better attend to the task at hand and so he turned to Matthew and asked, "Son, where is God?"

Matthew was only 5 years old and wasn't quite sure how to respond to Father's question, so he just looked blankly at the priest, which prompted Father to ask again, but in a louder, stronger voice," Son, I asked you, *WHERE IS GOD?!*"

Matthew became alarmed at Father's question and the tone of his voice and fled from the table. He ran into Luke's room and with terror in his eyes said, "Luke! Luke! God is missing and they think we've got him!"

Marriage

If you are called to be a husband, your vocation is the Sacrament of Matrimony. There is more to marriage than you being Prince Charming and living in the palace with your bride. In order to receive this Sacrament, you must be in the state of grace; that is you must be free of mortal sin.

Husband and wife spend their time together on earth striving to get each other to Heaven. They are to comfort and support each other, and be faithful until death. The purpose of marriage is to have children, raise them in the Catholic Faith and to grow in unity together.

If your calling is to marriage, it is very important that you marry a Catholic. The Catholic Church does not forbid mixed marriages (between a Catholic and a person from a different religion) but greatly encourages Catholics to marry other Catholics. In mixed marriages, the difficulties about faith and the very meaning of the Sacrament of Matrimony can become sources of great tension and disunity in marriage, especially as regards the education of children.

Those who feel called to marriage should pray that God directs the choice. Important people to ask for advice are parents and a parish priest.

The couple should receive the sacraments of Communion and Confession regularly to keep their hearts and souls clean. This will help them in hearing God's intention for them. You will be able to tell what the girl's character is like much better if you are going to Mass together and are including her at your family's dinner table.

It is very important to remain pure before marriage. This can be difficult in this culture where the majority of young people choose to "try on marriage" by living together before the wedding. This is why, again, the couple will need to be in agreement and work together to keep each other pure. Both the man and the woman will give their intended a wonderful and lasting gift of their purity if they wait until their vows are spoken in the Sacrament of Matrimony. You will see, it is worth it!

You and your spouse will receive sacramental graces to live out the vocation of marriage. This grace comes only from receiving the Sacrament of Marriage. This is another reason why it is very important to follow Holy Mother Church and Her guidelines for marriage.

> **You will be given extraordinary help for all that will come with marriage and family when you receive the Sacrament of Marriage in the Catholic Church.**

Once a man and a woman marry, they must welcome children. If couples are not blessed with children, God may have other plans for them such as adoption, or even work in charity. Again the sacramental graces will be given for whatever it is God has planned for the couple.

Okay, boys, there's a lot for which a father and husband is responsible. The father is the head of the household which means he has authority and wisdom from God to see that the family is going in the right direction. He must help his wife discipline and teach their children not only the Faith, but also manners and how to get along with others.

When God made Adam, He gave Adam the responsibility of taking care of the Garden of Eden. So from day one, man was made to work. Work supports the dignity of the person and helps man feel worthwhile. Just as Adam was to keep the Garden of Eden, so too today man is to work.

As a husband and father, it will be your responsibility to work for your family and provide all that they need to live, including a home, food, clothing and education. This doesn't mean that mothers can't work outside the home too to help bring in money for the family. It means that  as a man, you are the main supporter of your family. The ideal situation is for the husband to be able to make enough money so that his wife may take care of their children. This is a very high calling for a mother and a privilege to be able to be in the home when the children are little. But, a husband and wife will always make this decision together and will make the best one for their family. If your vocation is to be a husband, it is a good idea to master a skill, learn a trade, or get a college education so that you can support your family.

Along with his wife, a man will help in educating their children. They will need to pass on their love for the Faith and all that it teaches. The mom and dad are also to give their kids an education in reading, writing, and arithmetic. This may be done through a Catholic school, home school, or public school. Whichever choice works for the family, the most important thing is that dad makes sure everyone knows their Faith. He should be sure everyone gets to Mass on Sundays and Holy Days and also to confession on a regular basis.

Dad will teach his sons to be men and his daughters what to look for in a husband if her vocation is married life. A real man loves his family, works for them, loves God, and is happy in his vocation. He will make sacrifices cheerfully. This means he will skip going to his own ballgame if his wife is sick. It means he will help change dirty diapers and vacuum the floor without complaining. You see, God has given a husband a very big job in marriage, but it is a good and joyful vocation if this is your calling.

Single Life

A man may not have a vocation to the priesthood, consecrated life, deaconate or the married life. Does that mean he's a loser and has no vocation? Of course not! Remember everyone has the call to know, love and serve God. If you have not been called to any of the above, you are called to be single.

There are many ways to live the vocation of being single. It is NOT the last choice of someone who couldn't find someone to marry. It is just as special as being married or any of the other vocations. Single men have jobs and careers. Some are called to care for their elderly parents or relatives. All singles are called to the virtue of purity.

There are many things that single people can do because they don't have families. An example would be to go on mission trips, or to give of their money and time to charities that help the poor. Singles may have more money and time to devote to these things because they are not the head of a family.

There are also men who do not have a vocation to the priesthood, religious life, or marriage but are called to be celibate for apostolic reasons. They may live with their family or wherever is convenient for professional reasons, or they may live together with other men in a home. Their vocation is to work in the world while also giving their lives to God. An example of this is Opus Dei.

Work honors the Creator's gifts and the talents received from him. It can also be redemptive.
CCC# 2427

Begin

End

Family and Friends

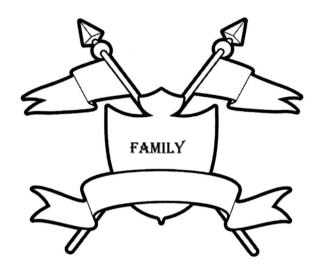

FAMILY

Just as God planned that you would be male, He chose your family. God picked your family for you. You may have both parents and annoying siblings or you may live with your grandmother and a couple of cousins. Remember that your dignity is not dependent on your circumstances. This doesn't mean, however, that God doesn't have a way to work things out for His good and the good of His people. That's actually what He does best for the people who love Him; He works things out for His good and theirs. And do you need to be reminded that His good is also your good? He always has a plan. Anyhow, your family is a gift.

It used to be that families had a "Coat of Arms" which was a certain design with symbols that belonged to the family. Family name and honor was very important. Kids cared about their family name and honor. That was their inheritance. As a son of God you have a royal family (and your inheritance is Heaven) but you also have an earthly family (and your inheritance is your family name). You should care about both and only want to bring honor to them. These are the things that should really matter to you.

Coat of Arms

There are lots of symbols that were used throughout history, which described a man and his family history, on his coat of arms. These symbols told of his virtues as well. You can make your own coat of arms that describes you and your family's traits.

Colors

> Gold: Generosity
> Silver or White: Peacefulness
> Red: Martyrdom or Military Strength
> Blue: Loyalty and Honesty
> Green: Hope
> Black: Grief
> Purple: Royalty
> Orange: Ambition

Fur

If a man's coat of arms was trimmed in fur, it marked dignity; usually the fur of ermine was used.

Symbols

Acorn: work the land
Anchor: hope
Angels: dignity
Antlers: strength and fortitude
Armor: leader
Arrow: ready for battle
Bat: awareness of the powers of darkness
Bear: strength
Beaver: perseverance
Boar's head: hospitality
Buck: will not fight unless provoked

Bull: bravery
Candle: life
Carnation: admiration
Castle: safety
Cat: vigilant
Crescent: honored by a sovereignty
Cross: Christianity
Dagger: justice
Dog: vigilant
Dolphin: love
Donkey: patience and humility
Dove: good tidings
Dragon: valor and protection
Duck: resourceful
Eagle: alert and high spirited
Elephant: good luck
Fire: zealous
Fleur-de-lis: purity
Fox: wisdom
Goose: resourceful
Grapes: liberality
Hammer: honor
Hawk: perseverance
Heart: affection
Inkhorn: educated
Jewel: supremacy
Keys: guardianship
Lamb: gentle
Lion: courage
Rose: grace and beauty
Sword: justice
Shield: defender
Wheat Leaves: faithful

Mom

Dude, here's a list to remind you of all that mom does for you, in case you've forgotten or haven't noticed. She:

- ✓ DRIVES YOU TO YOUR ACTIVITIES
- ✓ PROVIDES YOU MEALS
- ✓ DOES YOUR LAUNDRY
- ✓ BUYS YOUR CLOTHES
- ✓ CLEANS THE HOUSE – TOILETS AND ALL -
- ✓ TEACHES YOU MANNERS
- ✓ TEACHES YOU RIGHT FROM WRONG
- ✓ LOVES YOU UNCONDITIONALLY
- ✓ GIVES YOU ADVICE
- ✓ PRAYS FOR YOU

The best thing your mom has given you is the gift of life. Moms are love. They aren't perfect but they do everything in their power to take care of their children.

Your mom rocks! She accepted you as her son and since she did that you have the opportunity to have eternal life in Heaven.

Because of this, she should be treated with respect and love.

Yeah, mom might yell and nag sometimes and get on your nerves at other times but face it, you love your mom. And you should!

You can tell a lot by how a guy treats his mom. Have you ever been to a friend's house and he talks back or mouths off to his mom? How do ya feel about it?? It should make you feel uncomfortable, like you want to tell your friend, *"Chill, out!"* That's because all moms deserve respect.

Remember, the 4th Commandment tells kids to honor their fathers and mothers. You see, God knows what will make you feel good and what will  make you feel bad. Seriously, when you speak poorly to your mom, how do you feel? Not good, right?

See, God knows! He just wants what is right for you and so He told you that you need to "Honor Your Father and Mother."

Need a role model?

Think of Jesus and His mother!

If you ever really question how amazing your mom is, go spend time with someone who has a little baby. Spend a few hours and see what it's like. You like the kid, sure, but are you willing to wipe his nose? Nah, but his mom is willing to because she loves him as only she can—which is a gazillion times more than you do. Moms love their babies more than anyone can imagine.

Dad

Dad, along with mom, has given you a family. He is your example of how to be a man. Although no family is perfect, some seem to do a better job at mirroring what God intended than others. The thing is, no matter what your family circumstances are, your own personal dignity does not change. Remember reading that in the beginning of the book? Well, it's true. So, if your dad does a lot of great "dad" things like fishing with you or teaching you how to throw a baseball, your dignity is the same as if he didn't. Sure, life is good when it has those things in it; but no matter what, you can grow up to be a man that matters. Chances are, your dad can teach you a lot of ways to be a man but because he isn't perfect, you might decide some things don't work. Even still, the 4th Commandment says to honor your father and that's what you ought to do. That's God's way of teaching you to be in obedience—even if it isn't easy.

In the Vocation section, you read all about marriage and the duties of fatherhood. That should give you a pretty good idea of what God expects from men who are fathers. They cheerfully make sacrifices for their family. For example, your dad may drive an old car so that he can afford your Catholic school tuition. He may not get to go on vacation because he pays for you to play hockey instead. Maybe your dad simply takes care of the everyday expenses of feeding and caring for a family. In the end a good father won't miss all these things because having and caring for you and your siblings is way more rewarding. Dads are real men that matter.

Brothers and Sisters

It sometimes seems like brothers and sisters get on your nerves. But as you grow up you will find that your siblings are your best friends. The family is where you learn to get along. Yeah, your brother messes up your room and takes your stuff or your sister always wants to hang around you and your friends and bothers you, but, when you are a man and have a job, you'll know how to get along with an annoying coworker because your annoying brother or sister taught you how!

 When you share your candy with your sister, you will grow up to be a generous man who gives to the poor. When you help babysit the little ones, you practice responsibility which will help you to be a good worker when you have a career. When you stand up for your sister you are learning to stand up for others, as well.

Siblings help you learn how to behave and what is important. When you do as your parents ask and practice kindness, generosity, or patience with your brothers and sisters, you are actually becoming a man that matters. Remember, God gave you your family for a reason. It was no coincidence, so look at your family as a way to help you become the man God wants you to be and help your siblings do the same. It won't happen overnight, but all Good things God has in store take perseverance, so persevere and be a good sibling!

Friends

You may have heard an old saying from your mom or grandma that goes, "Birds of a feather flock together." Sounds cheesy, but hey, it's true. People with the same likes, dislikes, hobbies, beliefs, opinions, and interests usually hang out together. It's easy to settle for anyone to hang with, but in reality, you have to be choosy about who your friends are.

1. TAKE YOUR TIME AND CHOOSE THE FRIENDS THAT ARE RIGHT FOR YOU. IF YOU AREN'T SURE ABOUT SOMEONE, CHANCES ARE HE ISN'T THE BEST CHOICE FOR A FRIEND.
2. IF YOU PICK THE WRONG FRIENDS, YOU MAY END UP IN TROUBLE.
3. MOVE ON AND GET NEW FRIENDS WHEN YOU SEE THE ONES YOU HAVE ARE MAKING BAD DECISIONS—BUT LET YOUR MOM OR DAD KNOW IF THEY ARE DOING SOMETHING DANGEROUS.
4. WHILE FRIENDS ARE GOOD TO HAVE, SOMETIMES A GUY JUST NEEDS TO BE ALONE WITH HIS THOUGHTS—MAKE SURE YOU DON'T OVERDO THE AMOUNT OF TIME YOU SPEND WITH OTHERS.

5. A GOOD FRIEND WILL RESPECT YOUR THOUGHTS AND OPINIONS AND YOUR FAMILY'S RULES.
6. ALL THE THINGS YOU LOOK FOR IN A FRIEND ARE ALSO THE THINGS YOU SHOULD GIVE TO OTHERS.
7. IT SOUNDS CHEESY, BUT YOUR GOAL IN LIFE IS TO GET TO HEAVEN AND YOU SHOULD PICK THE SORT OF FRIENDS WHO WILL HELP YOU GET THERE.
8. YOU'VE GOTTA BE THE KIND OF FRIEND WHO HELPS HIS FRIENDS GET THERE, TOO!

> **A good friend isn't perfect but he does help bring out the best in you... and you do the same for him. It's that simple.**

Beat the Bully

Sometimes people think of the bully as someone like "CJ," the big gangster type of guy who intimidates and beats up people. Yeah, this is one type of bully, but more commonly, bullies are the guys that get by the radar of teachers, principals, and other adults. They can be sneaky and conniving. You know the type.

He teases constantly, he name calls and belittles, but says he's joking. He trips you in the hall and laughs, he makes fun of your haircut or clothes all the while smiling and being polite to the adults. Bullying takes on many forms.

Face it, you could try to beat the bully at his own game by doing the same things back, but is that the best thing to do? Think about it, the biggest reason guys bully is because they are insecure and want to make themselves feel big. Lots of things can make a guy feel insecure:

- FAMILY PROBLEMS
- NOT BEING SMART
- BEING OVERWEIGHT
- BEING UNDERWEIGHT AND NOT "BUFF"
- BEING POOR
- JUST NOT LIKING HIS OWN LOOKS

The bully has issues. Here's what you can do:

1. REMEMBER THAT EVEN BULLIES ARE LOVED BY GOD.
2. REMEMBER YOUR OWN WORTH; YOU'RE A COOL GUY, A PRINCE ACTUALLY.
3. REMIND YOURSELF THAT THE BULLY HAS ISSUES.
4. PRAY FOR HIM.
5. STAY AWAY FROM HIM.
6. MAKE SURE YOU TELL AN ADULT IF A BULLY HAS CAUSED HARM TO SOMEONE – AND REMEMBER THAT HARM CAN BE PHYSICAL BUT CAN ALSO BE EMOTIONAL. IF YOU AREN'T SURE THAT A BULLY HAS CROSSED THE LINE, YOU NEED TO SPEAK UP!

7. STAND UP FOR YOURSELF. TELL THE GUY TO *"GET LOST!"* OR *"GO BE A JERK SOMEWHERE ELSE!"*
8. DON'T LET ANYONE MAKE YOU—OR SOMEONE YOU KNOW—THE VICTIM.
9. LET THE BULLY KNOW YOU DON'T CARE WHAT HE THINKS—AND THE SAME GOES FOR HIS FRIENDS.
10. SAY THINGS—OUT LOUD OR EVEN TO YOURSELF—SUCH AS, *"I CARE WHAT YOU THINK BECAUSE...?"* OR *"I'M NOT AFRAID OF YOU!"*

If you're the bully you better tell yourself that one day this "nerd" could be your boss. Then you need to go to confession and start over.

Girls

Maybe you're at the stage where you're saying, "Yuck, girls!" or you might be thinking, "She's cute." Wherever you are, here's the deal, guys: girls are different than you and they think differently than you.

The best way to socialize at this stage of your life is with families and groups of friends. Most of the time if you go to an event where there are girls, they'll be doing the giggling and whispering thing and following you and your friends at a distance. You see, since the feminist movement, girls have become more and more, shall we say, forward. It was once the role of the boy to do any initiating toward girls. You can get back to that. If a girl is "chasing you," politely, always politely, let her know you're not interested. If she texts you, don't text back; if she calls, don't answer—you get the picture. This sends a loud message: *"NOT INTERESTED!"*

Chances are she just doesn't know any better. She is probably getting most of her advice from her dingy friends or magazines. Just remember to always be kind. Since you are becoming a man that matters, you will find that in these situations, you can help a girl understand her own dignity by not responding to any of her inappropriate (silly or "forward") behavior. That is a very noble thing for you to do.

Your parents will decide when and how you socialize with girls. You can always ask your sister and your mom for advice, since they are girls and know how they think. Talk with dad too, since he's been through it.

Things to know about girls:

> Most girls are sensitive when it comes to boys. They get embarrassed and their feelings get hurt easily.
> Most girls grow into adults faster than boys.
> If you are nice to a girl, she may think you like her. Lots of girls read into everything. It is a good idea to be around other people when girls are present.
> Girls talk a lot and love to talk about themselves.
> Most of the giggling and whispering are about boys.
> Girls do stupid things when they spend the night with their friends, like call boys and try to embarrass their friends.
> If you can get a word in edgewise, you can talk to girls and they won't bite.
> Lots of girls are moody and their feelings change from minute to minute. They have a hormone thing going on.

- Some girls are drama queens and make a big deal out of everything.
- Girls like it when boys are respectful to them and have good manners.

Chivalry

Remember when you were a kid and your folks would read you stories about St. George and the dragon, or King Arthur and the Knights of the Round Table? Well, anyway, those were the times of heroes and damsels in distress. You see, it was way cool to be a knight and it was no easy task becoming one. There were steps and stages he had to go through. The knights were real men with character and faith. There was a whole code they had to live by. This included the manners they used in their homes and the respectful way they treated women.

Chivalry was the code a knight lived by and there were guidelines for winning a lady's affection. The knight had to prove his love to her by doing heroic deeds and services for her. He was gentle and kind to all women. In those days, all Christians were Catholic and the knights had a high respect for the women because of Our Lady whom they loved so much. This was then turned toward all women.

You can learn from the knights. You can strive to live by a code, the code of being a gentleman. Think of all girls and women like you do the Blessed Mother.

Here are some pointers you can start practicing with your sisters and your mom:

- ☩ Open doors for girls and let them walk in first. Never open a door, walk through it and let it close in a person's face.
- ☩ Walk beside girls, not in front of them, leaving them in the dust. When walking with a girl on a sidewalk, you should be closest to the street. This is from the days of chivalry when horses would trot by and men protected women from getting splashed.
- ☩ Don't use crude language or tell dirty jokes.
- ☩ Ditch the potty talk.
- ☩ Never pass gas in front of girls, instead excuse yourself and go into the bathroom.
- ☩ Open and close car doors for girls and women.
- ☩ It is **NEVER** okay for a boy to hit a girl or a man to hit a woman. Yes, your sister can get you awfully mad, but you are **NEVER** to touch her.

It is important for a nice guy like you to learn to guard his eyes. There are girls and women everywhere, at the store, at the pool, and even at church, who do not dress modestly. Make sure you do your best to keep your eyes on the girl's face. Unfortunately, girls can be clueless about how they dress but that doesn't mean you have to be!

As you get older, you'll be glad you got in the habit of guarding your eyes. This should be done when watching TV and movies, too.

You Got A "mazing" Skills?

Start

End

Your Guardian Angel

Joey Hunter was playing at his family's farm on a Sunday afternoon. The property was rather large, surrounded by woods and a creek. At 10 years of age, Joey loved to explore and collect things from nature. On this particular day, he drifted off to the farthest area of the property, when suddenly he felt a sharp sting on his right foot. He had been bitten by a poisonous snake, which still had its teeth holding onto Joey's foot. Joey shook his foot with all his might and hit the snake's head with a stick. Finally the snake let go and went away.

At this point, Joey knew that this type of snakebite was deadly and that he had to be taken to the hospital in a hurry. He knew he had to make it 150 yards to get back to the farmhouse in order to get help. By now, his foot was already swollen and purple and an excruciating pain was going up his leg. How was he going to make it?

Joey's mom was in the living room when she heard Joey screaming while at the same time crawling up the porch steps. His mom and dad rushed him to the hospital, where he was treated. By now, Joey's different organs had started to shut down and he was in a coma. Joey spent 9 weeks in the hospital before he was able to return home where he would finish his recovery.

When talking about the incident, his parents told him how surprised they were that Joey had made it 150 yards to the farmhouse in such a condition. He told them: *"I didn't walk myself; it was a young man, dressed in white, who carried me all the way to the porch steps."*

Joey had always had great devotion to his Guardian Angel and they believe that the *young man dressed in white* was truly Joey's Guardian Angel, since nobody saw anybody else at the farm property that afternoon.

Yes, angels are as real as you and I. They are pure spirits, which means that they don't have bodies, but they have intelligence and free will.

When you were born, God placed an angel at your side to protect you and guide you through your life on earth. God has done this for everyone.

 These are called "Guardian Angels." Their main job is to help you get to Heaven, by keeping you away from sinning. God expects you to make good decisions and to learn and grow in your relationship with His son, Jesus Christ.

God gives you a guardian angel to help you with many things. Guardian angels:

- Help us see temptation and say "no" to it.
- Protect us from danger to our soul and body.
- Offer prayers for us to God.
- Comfort us at the time of death.

You need to treat your Guardian Angel as you treat a friend. First of all, it's a good idea to give your Guardian Angel a name. That way you will be referring to him with more closeness.

Your Guardian Angel works 24/ 7 to help and protect you:

- Ask for his help before a test.
- If you need to deal with a difficult person, ask that person's Guardian Angel to help you—you will see a huge difference!
- You have to call your coach to tell him you can't make it to the game; ask your Guardian Angel to help give you courage so you can make the phone call.
- When you are having a hard time making a decision, ask your Guardian Angel for wisdom.
- When you get in trouble because you did something you weren't supposed to, ask your Guardian Angel for courage to accept the responsibility and set things right.
- Before a sports competition, ask for his assistance to help make sure nobody gets hurt.
- Ask your Guardian Angel to help you get up right away in the morning.
- When you feel pressure from your peers to do something that's not right, entrust yourself to your Guardian Angel immediately. Along with your own free will to do the right thing, he'll help you get out of the situation.

Did you notice that there isn't anything that you can't ask of your Guardian Angel?

Well, there isn't!

You probably learned the Guardian Angel prayer when you were little; if you haven't, it's never too late to learn it:

Angel of God, my guardian dear
To whom His love, commits me here
Ever this day, be at my side
To light and guard, to rule and guide. Amen

Get in the habit of reciting this prayer in the morning and before going to sleep at night. Say it also during difficult times. The more you grow in friendship with your Guardian Angel, the better he knows you and the better he is able to help you! And while your Guardian Angel can't stop you from using your free will as you choose, your Guardian Angel can help you live your life more fully for Christ if you allow him.

Beside each believer stands an angel as protector and shepherd leading him to life.
CCC# 336

Joseph of Nazareth

Saint Joseph is one of the greatest saints even though the Bible tells us very little about him. Did you know that there is no word of him recorded in the Gospels? It's not that he never talked, but most likely he was a silent person because in order to listen to God, one has to keep interior silence. God chose Joseph for one of the most important missions on earth: to look after Jesus and Mary. Wow! Can you imagine?

St. Joseph is the Patron Saint of the Universal Catholic Church. He lived a very holy life, and the amazing thing is that his life was very ordinary, like yours. He spent his days working to make a living and enjoying family time. Here are some of the reasons why he is so amazing, but also so down to earth:

- ✝ His life revolved around Jesus and Mary, whom he loved with all his heart. He made sure they were safe, had food to eat, and a warm home. His great love for them was shown by his generosity and self-giving.
- ✝ He had a lot of courage, especially when he had to take Jesus and Mary and flee to Egypt because Herod was trying to find the baby to kill him.
- ✝ He was obedient and trusted God when trials appeared, overcoming his fear.
- ✝ He was a just man, committed to his family.
- ✝ He was a humble man. When Simeon took baby Jesus in his arms at the Temple and recognized him as the Messiah, Joseph didn't go around bragging that he was the foster father of Jesus. He kept this joy in his heart, praising God.
- ✝ He was a carpenter and handyman and he was good at it because he didn't rush through his work; he finished each job well and with patience. He taught Jesus how to use the tools and build things. Later on, when Jesus was grown up, he was called "the carpenter's son," because he had learned the trade from his father Joseph.

Saint Joseph is a great example for men who want to grow in holiness through their ordinary lives. His feast day is March 19th. Ask St. Joseph to help you become a man that matters!

This Saint Joseph Prayer is said to be over 1900 years old...

O St. Joseph,

whose protection is so great, so strong, so prompt before the Throne of God, I place in you all my interests and desires. O St. Joseph do assist me by your powerful intercession and obtain for me from your Divine Son all spiritual blessings through Jesus Christ, Our Lord; so that having engaged here below your heavenly power I may offer my thanksgiving and homage to the most Loving of Fathers.

O St. Joseph,

I never weary contemplating you and Jesus asleep in your arms. I dare not approach while He reposes near your heart. Press him in my name and kiss His fine Head for me, and ask Him to return the kiss when I draw my dying breath. St. Joseph, Patron of departing souls, pray for us.

Amen

How to Make a Bow and Arrow

(Do this project with an adult and only use your bow and arrow in a safe place and with an adult's permission. Be smart!)

Once upon a time, the bow and arrow were used as weapons and for hunting. Many states today still have bow hunting. Use the directions here to make your own bow and arrow.

Bow

Step 1 Choose a piece of hard wood such as oak, hickory, or teak about one yard in length. It should be dead and dry and without knots or twists.

Step 2 You will need to identify the curve of your stick. This will be important later.

Step 3 Shape your bow, making it thicker in the center for strength and for the handle. Use a knife to shave off the wood inside the curve of the stick.

Step 4 Cut half moon notches 1-2 inches from the ends of the bow on the outside.

Step 5 String your bow with something like rawhide, or hemp cord. Attach the string in the notches of the bow by tying it tightly.

Arrows

Step 1 Find thin, straight sticks that are dead and dry. They should be half as long as your bow.

Step 2 Whittle the wood smooth on the arrows. Carve a small notch at the back end of each arrow that will be used with the bow.

Step 3 Make arrowheads. You can whittle the end of the arrow to a point or you can make a head from metal, stone, or glass. Any sharp piece will do. Cut a notch in the tip of the arrow and slide in the arrowhead. Secure it by wrapping it with string or cord.

Step 4 Glue some feathers onto the back ends of the arrows. This improves the arrow's flight.

Step 5 Make a target and put it on a tree that has a large trunk or on the side of an old building. You want your target in a place where there is area on each side— just in case you miss and your arrow goes flying off somewhere.

Body

What about
That Body
God
Gave You?

You've been reading a lot about the immortal soul and the things that make a difference in how you should live your life on earth so that you will enjoy eternity in Heaven. But remember that you are also that "body" which God gave you. Be aware of it and take care of it.

When a boy turns into a man, it is a process, a stage you go through. You will notice changes in your body, such as:

➤ Facial hair
➤ Underarm hair
➤ Pubic hair
➤ More hair growth on your legs
➤ Body odor and increased sweating
➤ Voice will become lower
➤ Hair and skin may become oily
➤ Skin may breakout
➤ Become stronger and more muscular
➤ Broader shoulders

These changes happen in your life when you are going through puberty. Everyone goes through it, but it happens at different ages for people. You can expect to see some of the above changes when you are between the ages of 10-18 years old.

Yeah, that's a big age range but it is because the changes usually happen slowly. This is all in God's plan for you to become a man.

Hormones, which are chemicals in the body, are being produced. They cause these changes. While these things are happening, it is a good idea to be aware of how to handle them.

**Hygiene sometimes seems scary
or a waste of time
but it is super important!**

Hair

It is essential for you to shower every day and use deodorant. You don't want to be stinky, do ya? Don't make your mom nag, **JUST DO IT**! Shampoo your hair daily to keep it from having that greasy look. Use a clarifying shampoo or shampoo for oily hair. This will keep you from dripping grease before noon! Ask your mom to get your shampoo from a salon. It costs a little more but it works better, lasts longer, and it doesn't flake. You don't want to have dandruff, do you?

Speaking of flakes...If you have a flaky scalp, aka, dandruff, use a shampoo with the ingredient coal tar or tea tree oil. They don't smell great, but man they work to get rid of flakes and itch. You can find them in the drugstore.

Newsflash!
What you look like and how you take care of yourself shows others how you feel about yourself.

Shaving

You can use a blade, just be careful not to nick yourself, or an electric razor. Whichever you choose, ask your dad to show you the best way to use it. Face it, your dad's been shaving a whole lot longer than you have—because you haven't yet—and his advice is worth heeding (that means taking).

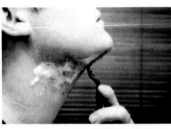

You can get really bad razor burn if you don't learn to shave correctly. Dad can show you which shaving cream works well for him and may have other tips or pointers to give you. No matter how young you are, when you get facial hair, it's a good idea to shave. You will look neat and clean. You won't have to shave very often at first; but as you get older your shaving will increase in frequency. When you do start shaving, don't leave your mom a big mess in the bathroom sink. Come on! She already has enough work to do. Make sure to rinse the sink and wipe the countertop after yourself.

You may want to use an aftershave lotion to neutralize your skin and make it feel cool and tingly. If your parents allow it, cologne can be used, but only a very little.

Guys today use way too much! Your cologne shouldn't arrive in a room before you do! Those around you can get bad headaches or the sneezes if a guy is wearing too much cologne. Subtle is the best, you know...less is more.

Skin

The skin is the largest organ of the body and it protects the insides of the body and eliminates waste. Hormones can cause you to have oily skin during puberty, which can cause breakouts. Usually breakouts are fairly easy to control, but sometimes a doctor's help is needed. This is something you and your parents have to decide, but the following tips are worth giving a try before heading to the doctor.

The skin can be regulated by proper care.

Here are some things you can do to help control breakouts:

- ➢ Change your pillowcase daily. Help Mom by throwing this in with your dirty clothes.
- ➢ Use clean towels and washcloths; help Mom by throwing them into the laundry daily. You can even offer to do some laundry if this becomes too much for Mom—but chances are she'll love your interest in staying clean!
- ➢ Limit or avoid greasy foods.
- ➢ Limit sugar and white flour foods.
- ➢ Increase drinking water and eating fruits and veggies.

Fast and Easy Skincare Steps for Guys

> ➤ Use a gentle water soluble cleanser. (Can you say "soluble" three times really fast?) Soluble means it dissolves easily in water.
> - o Do not use soap. It will actually cause you to breakout more!
> ➤ Use a gentle moisturizer.
> ➤ Use good quality products.
> - o Avoid the harsh toners, they only make things worse.

Dental Hygiene

This may seem like a no brainer, but dude, brush your teeth and floss. Go to the dentist twice a year for a checkup. If you wear braces, you may need to brush after every meal just to be sure you don't gross out everyone around you!

Do it for Mom

Every mom out there wants her son to become a man that matters. Want to know what every Mom wishes her son would do?

Well, even if you don't want to know, here it is:

- ✟ Say your prayers.
- ✟ Wipe the seat after you pee and put the seat down, then *WASH YOUR HANDS!*
- ✟ Keep your mouth closed when you chew. That means don't talk with food in your mouth, either.

- ✞ Wipe your hands on a napkin at dinner—not your shirt, pants, or tablecloth.
- ✞ Don't reach for the food across the table; politely ask to have it passed to you.
- ✞ No brainer...use silverware when eating.
- ✞ Pick up your stuff after you use it.
- ✞ Change into your pajamas before going to bed—don't get into bed with dirty clothes on.
- ✞ Wear clean clothes every day.
- ✞ Follow all the hygiene instructions above.
- ✞ Say "Please," and "Thank you," to adults.
- ✞ Greet adults with a firm handshake and smile.
- ✞ Talk to your mom; give her hugs.
- ✞ Get off the computer, TV, or video game right when you are asked to—and do it without complaining.
- ✞ Don't pick your nose. EVER!
- ✞ Don't wipe snot on your shirt sleeve.
- ✞ Change your underwear and socks every day.
- ✞ Tell the truth, no matter what, because you are becoming a man that matters.
- ✞ Do your homework and study hard.
- ✞ Don't fight with your brothers and sisters.

> If momma ain't happy, ain't nobody happy!

This list could go on and on, but you get the picture.

What would you add to this list?

Sports

Lots of guys play
sports and you may
be one of them. Or, if
you aren't, you may
want to consider
starting because of all
the benefits that can
be had from sports.

There really is something great about the challenge of a grueling game of soccer or the way you feel after running down the basketball court. This is because playing sports often puts your body to the test, makes you feel good about pushing yourself, and is a great way to stay in shape.

To be a good sports player means that you understand how to warm up your body so you don't get injured as easily as you could otherwise—without warming up— but also that you know the limits of what you are able to do. So, you can't leap tall buildings in a single bound, but you can, and should, be able to train your body to perform really well during any sports activity that you may play.

A sport is a way for a young
man's developing body to
get in shape and stay in
shape. When you are in
good physical shape—this
doesn't mean you have
ripped abs and 25" pecs—
you feel better about yourself.

This is because your body is made up of different chemicals called endorphins which get released when you participate in a challenging game of tennis or by throwing a football around. Endorphins help you feel good. You just won't get the same feeling being a couch potato and playing video games! Of course, for your sports to fully benefit you and your development, you need to eat right and sleep well. You can't push your body to play a tournament game of hockey if you haven't been eating the right kinds of food or getting enough sleep.

Face it, God created your body to work well but expects you to be smart about taking care of it so that it will last a lifetime. So, play sports, eat right, sleep well, and get on track with a basic combat training plan for your prayer life today.

Kicked up a Notch

As Pope John Paul II explains, a vocation happens day by day. This is exactly how it happened for Chase Hilgenbrinck. Chase retired recently from the New England Revolution Major League Soccer team to become a priest for the diocese of Peoria. Chase said that he thought about being a priest for many years and it was on his mind every single day. Chase grew up Catholic and attended Catholic schools. After Mass on Sundays, his parents would take his brother and him to pray in front of the statue of the Blessed Mother. They would pray specifically for the boys' future spouses. They couldn't have asked for a better spouse for Chase: the Holy Catholic Church! For Hilgenbrinck, "it's about Him, not me." Chase is excited to administer the sacraments and to give glory to God. Chase has definitely been "kicked up a notch" in careers!

Riddle Match

Match the questions (1 to 8) to the right answers (A to H) to complete the riddles.

1. What building has the most stories?
2. What can you see in the water that never gets wet?
3. In what place does Thursday come before Wednesday?
4. What can you keep taking and still leave behind?
5. What can you put inside a barrel to make it lighter?
6. What eats but never swallows?
7. What gets wetter and wetter the more it dries?
8. What has wheels and flies, but is not an aircraft?

your reflection | holes | the library | garbage truck
towel | rust | the dictionary | footsteps

Work Your Brain Cells...

1. Do you know what is as light as a feather but no man can hold it for long?
2. You can take away the whole and still have some left or you can take away some and still have the whole left. What is it?
3. A palindrome is a word that is spelled the same forwards and backwards, like "bib." Check out these and see how many more you can come up with: RACECAR, LEVEL, ROTOR, and EYE.

Answers are in back of book

Know Your History

Your History as a Catholic

Wherever you go, whatever you do, do it well because you are a Catholic! God's love for His Church is immense, as is His love for you. He's brought you, through baptism, into His Church and the great things about the Church's history are things for which you should feel proud.

When you introduce yourself to someone, extend a firm handshake, knowing that you represent God and His kingdom on earth. As a Catholic there is a cloud of witnesses about you that includes many people who have contributed greatly to Western Civilization.

So, when you extend a handshake to someone, make sure you realize all those who are with you and who have used their gifts from God to make this an awesome world.

Here's just a small list:

✚ Father Francisco de Vitoria is called the Father of International Law because he cared about human rights and countries being good neighbors. Father de Vitoria lived in the 16th century.

✚ The Catholic Church, along with the Pope, was very involved in developing universities and granting degrees so that education and knowledge could be shared all through Christendom. This was especially true during the time called the "Dark Ages," which really wasn't so dark, but you have to know your history to know how important the Church was during those times.

✝ Spanish Catholic theologians from the fifteenth and sixteenth centuries were very important to the way people today understand and learn about economics.

✝ Just as Jesus wanted, the Catholic Church has ALWAYS encouraged people to take care of the less fortunate—and to do it because every person has dignity and should be cared about—and not for fame or recognition.

✝ The Catholic Church tutored the barbarians who conquered Rome in the third and fourth centuries because the Catholic Church understood that the barbarians would never change their ways of plundering and killing until they understood the Gospel of Jesus Christ.

✝ Catholic thinkers from the twelfth century began talking about "natural rights" so when you read the Constitution of the United States where it says, "We hold these truths to be self evident, that all men are created equal...," well, that comes from YOUR faith!

✝ Father Boscovich, who lived in the eighteenth century, was amazingly smart about planets and their orbits. He wrote a book called "The Theory of Natural Philosophy" that made a big difference in science and studying planets.

✝ For many hundreds of years, Benedictine Monks worked hard to till land and create ways to transport water when no one else would. They turned swamp lands into great fields that provided food and they even became leading producers of iron by the thirteenth century.

Check out how this list includes some names and then just some groups. That's because we will never know all the names of the Catholics who worked so diligently for God and helped build up the world. Maybe one day you'll be famous in the world, but maybe you won't. The thing about working for God is that you'll always be famous to Him!

So, next time you meet a new person, extend your hand and offer a firm handshake and remember that you are surrounded by all these Catholic brothers who have lived before you and who are your friends in Christ.

On the Other Hand...

Circumstances that have happened in the past can be repeated when lessons haven't been learned.

There is an interesting proverb that says, "A smart man learns from his own mistakes but a wise man learns from the mistakes of others." That's pretty darn powerful if you think about it. We all want to be smart and learning from our own mistakes is a good start, but God loves when people are wise and that means we need to learn from other people's mistakes—and that involves learning history.

Not only that, but you should be knowledgeable about what has gone on in the world. God gave you a brain to use and learning history is really quite interesting.

When you are a man and able to vote, knowing history can help make a difference in the future.

Besides, some of the best stories come from history and are very interesting. In some schools today true history is not taught. Things get changed and stories grow. So, it is up to you to read things that the Church teaches and learn so that you will grow into a responsible citizen.

You can make a real difference if you are informed and knowledgeable. But you always have to be on guard to make sure what you learn isn't against your faith as a Catholic.

Let's take a look at one of the dictators that lived and ruled in the last century or so. His name is Adolph Hitler. He took power in Germany several years after the First World War was over.

Things were not so good in Germany. There was unemployment and inflation. The German people were ready for a change, for a fresh start. Along came Adolf Hitler, who was likeable and gave mesmerizing speeches on how great the German people were and how Germany deserved to be prosperous and powerful. He said what people wanted to hear and so they kept listening. Who can blame them? Who doesn't want to hear that their life is supposed to be awesome and amazing? You do, right? But knowing it is awesome and amazing because of God, so you can serve God, is way different from seeing *yourself* as awesome and deserving amazing things separate from God.

Anyhow, Hitler had it out for certain people like Jews, Catholics, Blacks, and people with disabilities. He wanted to rid Germany of any of these "unworthy" people. He made movies that made people feel sorry for the old and those with disabilities. These movies made people believe that it was better for those kinds of people to be killed than to live! Sounds crazy doesn't it? This is called mercy killing, which we know is a terrible sin.

Do you know why this is a sin to kill anyone, regardless of how sick or helpless he or she may be? It is a sin because God gave that person life and only God can take it from that person. Others are not supposed to do that. Soon, millions of people who lived in Germany during this terrible time in history were killed. This is called the "Holocaust."

The Catholic bishops and the Holy Father tried to reason with Adolf Hitler and begged him to stop what he was doing. They even smuggled many Jews and others out of danger, through the Vatican. Because the priests, bishops, and the Pope spoke out against his plan, Hitler had many Catholics, clergy, and nuns killed along with the Jews, who had become scapegoats – that means the ones who were blamed for everything.

We look back, now, and ask, "How could this have happened?" Millions of people were killed.

Well, it happened slowly, over time, and it was subtle enough so that people didn't realize they were being brainwashed through movies, newspapers and speeches.

This is where knowing history comes in. Can you think of any group of people right now who have no rights at this time, right here in your country? Think hard.....

 The unborn babies have no rights to protect themselves if their mothers do not want them. Right now, in this country, it is legal to murder unborn babies. How did this happen?

First of all, years ago women were told their rights were more important than an unborn baby's rights. Soon the words "unborn baby" were not used to describe a pregnant woman's child. The baby was called, 'the product of conception," or "a bunch of cells." Eventually, in many people's minds, unborn babies were not really even people. It's just like the Jews or the disabled during that time in history in Germany. It seems unbelievable, but in just a few years people can be made to believe lies. If you aren't sure about this, remember that you were once an "unborn baby." Aren't you glad your Mom decided to deliver you?

This is why it is so important to know your history and your Faith. It has been around for over 2000 years and has not changed its teachings. You can count on the Catholic Church to know what is right and true even when people become confused. Anything you want to know about can be found in the *Catechism of the Catholic Church.* It's not like a book you will sit down and read cover to cover; but when you have a question about what is right or wrong, that's where you'll find the answer.

In fact, if there's been anything on your mind, now is the time to get answers! Ask your mom or dad to help you look through the Catechism. You will be amazed at the amount of information there. It is because the Catholic Church was founded by Jesus and still teaches the things Jesus came for us to know.

Back to the whole brainwashing idea... What Hitler did in Germany during the 1930's and 40's is being done here and now. Not by a dictator, but by Hollywood. Yup, that's right. Hollywood makes movies that are emotional to make people feel and react a certain way. Old people are made to look pathetic and worthless. People commit suicide and it's made to look heroic. You know, stuff like that. This is how a whole society can change.

You gotta have your head on straight. Know your history and know your Faith so that you will be able to tell when movies or shows try to push a way of thinking that is not right and is against what the Church teaches.

YOU CAN'T ALWAYS GO WITH THE HERD WHEN YOU GO WITH GOD!

Do you see what I see?

1. Concentrate on the four small dots in the middle of this picture for about 45 seconds.
2. Now look at an empty area of a wall.
3. Give yourself a few seconds and then start blinking a couple of times.

Get the Facts

Sometimes history gets mixed up because of those writing about it. Many times these people have their own opinions and it influences how they record events. One example of this is the Spanish Inquisition.

You might ask: Why would someone write things that are not true? Well, they have a strong opinion and want others to have it, too. This is why, again guys, you gotta know the facts. Always read history from a good Catholic source along with any of your other sources. At least you will get information that isn't all one-sided.

Well, anyway, do you remember Queen Isabella of Spain? She's the queen who sold her jewels to buy Columbus three ships for his expedition in which he found the "New World."

She is known as the Catholic Queen. Her husband, Ferdinand, convinced the Holy Father to allow him to have an inquisition in Spain. Ferdinand was concerned with the many teachings that were being spread that were considered false and that jeopardized the Catholic Church.

This inquisition was controlled by the monarchy but followed all the procedures set up by the Holy See. The Holy See is where the Pope is. An inquisition is an institution set up by the Church to combat heresy, or false teachings. There have been many of these throughout history.

Heresy was considered a crime and was punished very severely. It was a matter of grave importance that people knew the true Faith because their immortal souls depended on it. You see, before the Reformation, everyone who was a Christian was a Catholic and the Church was very protective of Her teachings so that the people would always have the truth. After the Reformation, there were so many splits in religion that the Church couldn't control all the heresy and it became very widespread.

It's kind of hard to understand in this day and age about heresy because there are so many religions, and in our society they are all tolerated. It may seem harsh to you that heretics, those who spread wrong teaching, were severely punished or killed, but that's just the way things were in those days. It's similar to how there was a time when people who had serious diseases would be sent away—that was how people protected themselves from all contracting the disease. In many ways we know better but in many ways we still do horrible things to one another. This is why we always need God's help.

Anyhow, those targeted by the Spanish Inquisition were Jews and Muslims. For many years the Spanish had fought the Muslims. Isabella and Ferdinand really wanted their country to be Catholic so they told all those who were not Catholic to either convert or "get out." Many of the targeted people left. Many had true conversions but there were those who did not. Some converted to gain political positions or to be able to stay living in Spain.

The Inquisition also set up trials for those accused of heresy. Most of the inquisitors, those officiating over the trials, had university degrees. The Catholic Church really wanted to make sure things were as fair as possible, but sometimes the people who ruled the land did whatever they wanted instead of what the Church wanted.

Many people were accused of heresy by their neighbors, but were found innocent and had no punishment. Others were detained in jail for long periods of time without even knowing what they were accused of or by whom. Their property was taken to pay for the trial. The prisoners were not allowed to attend Mass or receive the sacraments. Some died in prison. It really was terrible and many innocent people were killed, along with ones who were guilty of the crime of heresy.

The Inquisition did use torture to get the accused to admit to their crimes. In the end, the accused could be severely punished or even burned at the stake. It is very difficult to find true statistics on how many people were killed or tortured during the Spanish Inquisition, but many scholars today say that the numbers people quote are very misleading.

What can you learn from all this? Well, one thing is quite certain; the Catholic Church is made up of sinners. No doubt throughout history there are lay people, priests, bishops, and even popes who have been terrible examples of what a true follower of Christ should be. This is sad, but true. But, ask yourself this...Even if the members of the Church are sinful, and we all are, does that mean that the teaching that Jesus gave the Catholic Church is wrong?

Does any bad action of a Catholic make the Church's teachings wrong? Fortunately, NO! You see, that's the thing; the Church has kept the teachings of Jesus for over 2000 years and has not changed Her beliefs.

Pope John Paul II was a great reconciler. This means that he often spoke words that helped people heal. Pope John Paul II knew that there were sinners in the

Church's history but he also knew that the Catholic Church was the Church that Jesus founded and even sinners couldn't take this heritage away.

This is why you put your trust in the Church, not in sinful individuals. Learning the history of the Church, the good and the bad, makes you better able to serve God and more able to partake in your heavenly citizenship.

The four marks of the Church are that she is One, Holy, Catholic, and Apostolic. This is your heritage on earth and in Heaven.

Buffalo Bill

Do you know who Buffalo Bill is? Maybe you've seen movies or read stories about him. He had a very colorful and exciting life. But did you know he was a Catholic? Surprised? Read on and see what else you can learn about him.

Buffalo Bill's real name is William Frederick Cody. He lived from February 26, 1846 until January 10, 1917 and was born in Iowa near Le Claire. Cody's father, Isaac, believed that Kansas should be a free state, and was opposed to slavery. Unfortunately, many folks in the area disagreed with Isaac. It was a violent time in those days, and, sadly, people who disagreed with William's dad formed a mob and stabbed him, trying to kill him. He was able to save his father and dragged him to safety. Isaac Cody was forced to leave home to keep from being killed. From that time on the Cody family was persecuted by the supporters of slavery. Isaac never fully recovered from his injury and died when William was only a boy. At age 11, Bill took a job delivering messages up and down the wagon train.

Soon after, Bill took a job as an unofficial scout for the Army. It was then he first received the title Indian Fighter. He earned this title when he saw an Indian shoot his friend and immediately raised his gun and fired at the Indian, who collapsed and landed in the river. At the age of 14, young Bill met a Pony Express agent who gave him a job building the way stations and Bill later became a rider.

From 1868-1872, Bill worked for the Army as a scout. Bill also gathered and killed buffalo for the Kansas Pacific Railroad. He killed 4,280 buffalo in only eighteen months, and that's how he got his name.

While stationed in a military camp in St. Louis, Missouri, he met Louisa Frederici. They married and had four children together.

After Buffalo Bill's career with the Army, he put together a traveling show called the Buffalo Bill's Wild West. You may recognize Annie Oakley, Wild Bill Hickok, and Frank Butler as some of the folks who were performers in the show. Buffalo Bill even had Sitting

Bull and a band of Indians in the show. These performances were known to be exciting and colorful. For 10 years this show traveled all over the world.

In the last years of Bill's life he began to think about his life. He gave up drinking all together and began to control "his passions." On his deathbed, suffering from kidney failure, he was baptized into the Roman Catholic Church.

Buffalo Bill died the day after his baptism into the Roman Catholic Church.

??? What Would You Do ???

Henri Mailliard was a young boy of 12 when his parents died of whooping cough, leaving him destitute with four younger sisters. Henri was a very intelligent boy, although often called "difficult" because of his constant questions. He really only wanted to spend time  learning by exploring and doing; he despised the manual labor of his father, a blacksmith. Henri hated everything about the shop his father had worked in: the smells, the heat, and the dirtiness of it all. Most of all, Henri resented that he was always forced to help.

Now, with his parents gone, he had a chance to start over. Henri felt a mix of sadness and excitement at the prospect. He had loved his parents, but the cruelty of life had hardened his heart. Now, with his parents gone, his sisters were to be sent to live with his aunt, his mother's sister. She was married to a wealthy man and was never blessed with her own children. They wanted to take in Henri, too, but everyone knew that he was just too difficult for these well meaning, yet inexperienced, parents. It was decided - off to the orphanage for him. But Henri had his own plan in mind.

Henri decided to run away. He had heard about New France and thought it sounded adventurous and exciting.

With a small bag packed and ready to go at a moment's notice, he watched the shipyards daily to gain information. He learned rather quickly that Samuel de Champlain was on his way to the New World. The war with Britain was over and Champlain was freed from the English and on his way back to Quebec. Henri knew he had no time to waste. That very day Henri, with the blackness of the night for his ally, stole away on Champlain's ship. Henri made his way down to the belly of the ship and hid.

Not many days into the journey, a crew man found Henri, seasick and cold, huddled in the dark corner of the underbelly of the ship. "What is this now?" asked the rough seaman, taking the boy to the captain. Henri was certain he would be thrown to the sharks. That was standard procedure for stowaways.

Lucky for Henri, Champlain was with the captain of the vessel. As the seaman threatened Henri with bodily harm, Samuel Champlain intervened and asked the boy some questions in his deep, gravelly voice, "What are ya doin here, garcon?"

Henri did his best to stop shaking and looked the captain straight in the eye. "I'm an orphan, sir, and looking to start a new life in a new land."

Champlain admired the boy's courage and with a twinkle in his eye said, "He'll come with me. I need a helper. We need a new mate on this ship. There's no reason to feed the sharks when we can get some work out of him."

The shipmates grumbled but knew better than to voice their displeasure. Henri gulped back his tears of gratitude and followed Champlain into the hull for food and water.

During the long voyage, Henri learned to read a compass and tie knots that would be valuable information in the New World. Champlain told Henri stories and taught him about trapping, shooting, and the languages of the Indians in the area of Quebec, which was the location of the colony.

All of this Henri learned very quickly and enthusiastically. In some ways this is what he had craved his entire, short life. He was free from his father's shop but often felt a deep sadness for his parents. Still, he couldn't wait to meet the Indians and to live his new life with Champlain, whom he now called Uncle Sam.

When they reached the New World, Champlain didn't want to take young Henri on the hunting expedition. Champlain feared the conditions would be too harsh for the young garcon. Uncle Sam decided to leave Henri with the Black-Robes, Jesuit priests who were living with the Huron Indians.

There were three Indian tribes living in the area: the Huron, the Iroquois, and the Mohawks. The Huron were always friendly to strangers. The Jesuits moved freely through the Huron villages of longhouses. Sadly, however, the French brought with them disease and sickness, which quickly spread to the villages, killing many Huron.

The French were interested in converting the Hurons to Christianity. What began with one priest baptizing a young brave continued with Father Isaac Jogues' work.

Father Isaac had been able to make progress and soon entire Huron families were asking for baptism. This meant that the Huron were now living a Christian lifestyle, much different from their enemies, the

Iroquois. That year, the Huron decided not to go on their annual hunting and trading trip because the enemy was infiltrating these areas. This was the year that Henri was left with Fr. Isaac.

Fr. Isaac, along with other Frenchmen and a group of Christian Hurons, decided to make the dangerous trip. They knew that without the supplies and medicine that they would get through trades, it would be a long year of suffering for the Huron. Knowing it was to be perilous, Henri begged to go with the Black-Robe. He longed to use his newly acquired skills and just as much as he longed for adventure.

Fr. Isaac prayed much before making his decision. He asked Henri, "Young man, are you baptized?"

Henri answered Father, "Oui."

Fr. Jogues questioned him further, "Do you love Jesus? Are you willing to die on this trip to bring back medicine and supplies to our Indian brothers and sisters?"

Henri, thoughtfully replied, "Fr. Isaac, I do not know if I love Jesus, but I do want to help the Indians because they have been good to me."

Father contemplated and prayed two days before telling Henri his answer. As Father prayed for the young Henri, God revealed to him that Henri would have a profound purpose in the New World. In answer to his prayer, God allowed Father to know that Henri should accompany them on the trading expedition. Father Isaac trusted God's answer and informed Henri that he would be able to travel with the group.

The small group, which fit into three canoes, left on their trip. Fr. Isaac offered Mass daily and provided Confession to all the baptized. Henri learned to serve at Mass for Father and became a close and trusted companion. Henri saw firsthand how much Father Isaac truly believed in and loved Jesus. At night, as they camped, Henri would ask Father questions about Jesus and the Church He founded. Father was well aware of the stirring in Henri's soul and prayed fervently for this orphan.

The group reached Three Rivers safely. Soon they were attacked by Mohawks, members of the Iroquois nation. Fr. Isaac had sent Henri to gather firewood nearby when they were ambushed. When Henri quietly returned, he saw what had happened. With the tracking skills he had learned from the Christian Hurons, Henri followed the captured group, staying away a safe distance. What Henri witnessed gave him nightmares for the rest of his life. The prisoners were forced to run the gauntlet, a game of torture used by the Mohawk. Two lines of braves, holding various objects with sharp edges, hit and beat the prisoners as the prisoners were forced to run through the two lines. They were beaten over and over until their skin was falling from their broken bones.

Henri hid and watched with tears streaming down his face. That night he crept into camp and found Fr. Isaac bruised and beaten. Henri wanted to help his beloved priest. But Father, fearing for the boy's life, sent him away.

Henri, being overwhelmed with grief, did not want to leave. Henri was afraid Father and the others would surely die. Henri had already lost his parents and he couldn't bring himself to imagine losing Father, too.

The hardness Henri had once felt deep in his heart was no longer there. It has softened with his love of Christ.

Remembering God's revelation to him, Fr. Isaac whispered to Henri, "You are destined to be used by God. You must not try to help me escape. The men here need me to pray with them through this terrible trial. If I escape, their immortal souls may be in danger. I cannot let them lose their faith now, not after all it has taken for them to accept Jesus. You must go now, my son. We shall meet again, if not in this world, in the next. In Nomine Patris, et Filius et Santus."

With the priest's blessing, Henri, face wet with tears, quietly stole away into the darkness. Henri Mailliard made it safely back to the Huron village. He lived with them and learned their ways. So inspired by Fr. Isaac, Henri returned to France as a young man, entered the Jesuits and worked to convert the Indians.

Henri never saw Fr. Isaac alive again but learned that Father had lived in slavery with the Iroquois until he eventually escaped to France. However, instead of staying in his safe homeland, Father Isaac eventually returned to New France to continue his missionary work, where he was ultimately killed by an Iroquois brave.

Father Isaac Jogues was born in 1607 and died in 1646. New France is now Canada. Father Jogues was one of the first martyrs on the North American Continent.

Catholic America

When our country was being settled back in the 1600's or so, there were not a lot of Catholics. This is because the first Americans were mainly English, and they were mostly Protestant. The French, who were mainly Catholic, settled in Canada.

It wasn't until the 1800's that Catholicism really grew in America and this was due to immigration and conversions.

Immigration is when someone comes into a country from another country – for whatever reason. Maybe they are trying to get a better life or maybe they want to practice their faith.

The Irish came to America by the thousands because their country was having hard times. They did this according to the laws in America and were proud to become American citizens. The Irish are strong Catholics and they brought their religion with them when they came to America.

Many other Catholic immigrants from Italy, Eastern Europe, Brazil, and Bavaria also came to the United States in the late 1880's and early 1900's. Maybe some of them were your relatives.

That is something to be very proud of and learn about!

Anyway, people from these countries not only brought their religion with them, but converted others as well. In order to convert someone, you must be a good "witness." People will look at you— what you believe and how you act—and think, "Hmmm...Joe makes me think being Catholic is the way I ought to be."

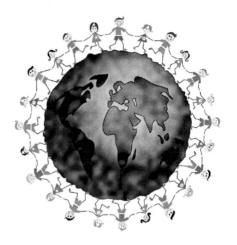

You see, that's what Catholics do, and that's how they help glorify God; they love and believe in their faith so much that they want others to have it, too, so they evangelize with their words and their actions and others convert to the Church that Jesus started. Today, the United States is about 25% Catholic.

There were challenges, though, during this time. The Church had to figure out how to take care of all these Catholics that had immigrated to America. Most important was to make sure that they could receive the Sacraments, which are necessary for a Catholic to receive God's grace. A deacon, priest, or bishop— depending on the Sacrament involved—administers the Sacraments. It is for this reason that the Church set up dioceses in America and sent bishops and priests to take care of the faithful.

The Catholics in America had some different ideas over the years that had to be corrected by the Holy Father. It seemed that lots of people in the U.S. slowly started to think that the Church should act like their democratic government. Some of the bishops thought that these modern ideas should pertain to the Church and how it operated. This, of course, is wrong because the Church was set up by Jesus to be run through the Apostles and their successors. It wasn't meant to change but to stay the same until Jesus comes back.

All the Catholic Church teachings should remain protected from heresy. Remember reading that heresy is when people start practicing their faith differently than the way it should be practiced? If everybody just does whatever they want, and thinks differently than the way Jesus taught, what kind of religion would that be?

Anyhow, the Holy Father—that's the Pope—had to correct the bishops and others who thought that the Church should be run like a democracy. In many ways, this challenge is still happening today.

But many good priests, nuns, bishops, and lay people are doing their best to help everyone stay faithful to the Magisterium, which is the teaching authority of the Church.

Another thing the Catholic Church had to deal with was the differences in the cultures. Catholics from Italy or Ireland or Eastern Europe have different traditions. Like any other family, the Church family had its squabbles amongst iself. If you go to larger cities, you will see parishes that were started in the different ethnic neighborhoods. That way they could have their own traditions and customs and still be part of the universal Catholic Church. See, the Church always works for the people.

There were other challenges, too. Catholics were persecuted by other Christian faiths. Remember, it was the Protestants that settled first in the New World. Many of them had an idea of how the United States should be and how everyone in it should be, as well.

They wanted their idea of a "Christian Country," and certainly many of those ideas were good, but they didn't understand Catholics and that caused problems. You see, many didn't appreciate the Catholic ways— like the Host being the actual body and blood of Jesus, or praying to the saints—and many Protestants were taught misinformation about what Catholics believed. Many Protestants didn't even consider Catholics to be Christians.

However, most Catholics were very tolerant of the religion of others. Anyway, a lot of this confusion and persecution led people like Elizabeth Ann Seton to form Catholic Schools, where all children were welcome and were taught about Jesus. By being kind and tolerant, the Catholic Church thrived in America and won many converts.

Remember, you represent the Church, too, as a Catholic guy. It is good to understand how much God loves you and then you can help others understand it, too. You can bring them closer to God and to the Catholic Church.

The Knights of Columbus

It was during this time that the Knights of Columbus was founded. Maybe you've heard of the Knights or seen them at an event in all their finery. Maybe your dad or grandpa is a Knight. Whatever the case, you gotta know about the Knights of Columbus.

Here's the deal: Fr. Michael McGivney founded the Knights of Columbus in 1882. He wanted Catholic men to have a membership in a society or union because at the time they were excluded from labor unions and were forbidden by the Church to join other organizations like the Masons.

(We'll talk more about the Masons later.)

So Father set up a group named after Christopher Columbus, since in those days Columbus was considered a real hero by Catholics because he brought the Faith to the New World. Anyway, the Knights were to be what's called a "mutual benefit" society. They set up insurance plans for widows and orphans. They were—and still are—all about helping people, just like Jesus has asked everyone to do.

The society also wanted to show that Catholics were patriotic and were good Americans. This actually happens to be totally what the Church teaches: to be a good citizen and care about your country.

The Knights were also able to bridge the differences between the ethnic groups within the Church. The Knights of Columbus did things like help families if the dad wasn't able to work because of an injury or illness. The Knights of Columbus are modern day heroes!

The organization of the Knights of Columbus has a structured hierarchy that you may one day want to learn about. But just so you know, now, it has levels that men can join and move up in rank. They also have a crest which every Knight wears as a lapel pin. The symbols include a shield, which represents medieval knighthood, and a cross, which represents Christ and His sacrifice. The anchor represents Christopher Columbus and the sword on their crest is to remind them of medieval times when the knight was on an errand of mercy. Remember the coat of arms you read about earlier in the book? Well, the Knights chose symbols that represented their beliefs and mission.

The Knights of Columbus, today, is the largest Catholic fraternal service organization in the United States. "Fraternal" means "brother." It's like a kind of boys club you may want to be part of when you get older.

They raise millions of dollars each year to give away to help others. They have a tradition of helping the disabled. One of the charities the Knights supports is the Special Olympics. They also give to pro-life causes. After the terrorist attacks of 9/11 they set up a "Heroes Fund" to give assistance to the families of firefighters, law enforcement officers, and other emergency workers.

Some famous Knights of Columbus have included Vince Lombardi, the former Green Bay Packers coach, and the baseball Hall of Famer, Babe Ruth.

What is a Mason?

Earlier, the Masons were mentioned. This is a "secret society" for men that Catholics are forbidden to join. This is because even though the Masons may do good deeds, they do not hold Christian beliefs. They have their own set of beliefs that go against Christianity.

Here's what Masons believe; be aware of these things and avoid these sorts of ideas and teaching:

- God is the master architect of the universe.
- There is a resurrection of the body.
- Man can achieve salvation by good works, not with God's grace.
- You don't have to believe in Jesus Christ or His Church for salvation.
- All religions are the same, whether Christian, Muslim, or Hindu and they can all explain the truth about God.

Okay, guys, here's where you need to be smart about your faith. The first couple of beliefs seem alright, don't they? And maybe that's how people get hooked in.

But you know better, right? You know that when it comes to the salvation of your immortal soul you cannot have the "two outa three ain't bad" mentality. Sorry dude, there is NO salvation outside of God's grace. So, even though the Masons may be nice guys and live moral lives, there's no going to Heaven without Jesus Christ and God's gift of salvation through Him. This is where they totally get off track. Jesus said there is only One Truth, so these guys are totally mixed up. Don't let them get you mixed up with them.

Here's why the Masons are considered a "secret society." They keep their beliefs and moral teachings secret. The Masons are required to swear an oath to God that they will NEVER tell the teachings of the Lodge or they will die a gruesome death, such as having their throat cut or their heart cut out. Real nice, huh? We know these things from those who have quit being Masons and have told us what really goes on. It's kind of like finding out about cults from members who left. When they are part of it they're all, *"Dude, this is great!"* but when they leave—escape—they're all *"It was terrifying and scary and mind controlling!"*

Anyway, those members that start out Christian slowly begin to put the beliefs of the Lodge ahead of their Christian beliefs and before they know it, they have lost their faith. This is why the Catholic Church forbids her members from joining the Masons. See, the Church is like a mother who protects her children. A Catholic man who has joined the Masons is not allowed to receive Communion. That's how seriously the Catholic Church takes this organization.

The teachings of the Masons are handed down secretly through rituals and oral tradition. The Masons have a pretty complicated organization. A high level Mason is called a Shriner. You may be familiar with them since they wear funny hats and drive tiny cars in parades and have the Shriner's Circus. They don't look harmful, right? In fact they seem to be doing a good thing. But that's why information is power. Now you've got it, you've got power!

You see, guys, the "end does not justify the means." Sometimes things are black and white, right or wrong, and there's no in-between. This is the case with the Masons. Even though they say they have charities, they are not good in the true sense of the word because they profess such grossly wrong teaching about God. No one or no group should ever try to convince you to put ANYTHING before God!

No matter how many good deeds groups like the Masons may do, it doesn't change the fact that they also believe and foster heresy and must be avoided.

This also applies to any other person or group of people who may be trying to pull you away from your family or your faith.

If that's ever the case—run for the hills!

Boys
in
the Kitchen

Lots of boys your age like to be in the kitchen, cooking. There are also a lot of guys who make a living as chefs. Food is good and fun and is a big part of the  American family and culture.

Here are a few basics on food. It is fuel for the body and God designed people to enjoy what they eat. The body is like a complicated machine, each system doing its own thing to make it function. Basic nutrition goes like this: if you eat less, you will burn the fuel and lose weight; if you eat more than you burn you will gain weight. As a growing young man you need to eat well, especially if you are playing sports, lifting weights or just being active outdoors.

Carbohydrates (carbs) are foods such as sweets, bread, pasta, potatoes, rice, chips, and crackers. They give you energy over the long haul, fuel to be burned. If you eat a lot of carbs and then go sit on the couch and watch TV or play video games this fuel is not burned up and turns to fat. So, even though you need energy, know that it's the carbs that will make you fat if you don't burn them off.

Proteins are the building blocks of muscle. A guy like you needs plenty of protein. You can find protein in eggs, meat, fish, nuts, cheese, and peanut butter. But a word of caution, make sure you don't have allergies to any of these things before you dig in!

Too much of anything, really, can make a person overweight, but you need protein to build your muscles. Again, if you are active in lifting weights, sports or just playing outdoors, you need protein.

Nutrients that are good for you are vitamins. Vitamins are found in fruits and veggies. Ya gotta eat each of these to be healthy.

However, lots of foods today do not have the nutrients in them for many different reasons you would find boring.

The point is, though, you need vitamins to keep you healthy. Ask your mom or dad about getting a multivitamin to make sure you get all the things you need to keep you feeling good. If you get plenty of vitamins—mostly through food but through a daily supplement if your parents think that is right for you—you will find that you feel great and don't get sick as often. But don't think you can take vitamins and not wash your hands and still stay healthy! It turns out that washing hands is one of the best ways to keep yourself well. *Wow, one more way your mom was right!*

Now for the fun part! Get in the kitchen, roll up your sleeves and try some of the yummy foods that follow. Make sure you ask Mom first and clean up everything when you are finished. Mom might throw a fit if you leave her a giant mess! Before you get started, be sure to wash your hands with soap and water – and make sure you have all the ingredients before you begin.

Homemade Mac and Cheese Is a Boy's Best Friend!

2 tablespoons butter; 1 tablespoon flour
1 – 1 ½ cup of whole milk; 8 ounces of sharp cheddar cheese, shredded; your favorite cheese can be substituted; 12 ounces of cooked noodles; shells are the best because they "cradle" the cheese

In a large, deep pan melt the butter. The heat should only be on medium so the butter doesn't burn. Once the butter is melted, sprinkle in the flour. With a fork, use the tines to both break up the flour and mix it completely into the melted butter. Make sure there are no lumps. This is called "rue."

Now turn the heat up to about medium high and pour in 1 cup of milk and keep stirring. Stir, stir, stir so that the milk comes up to a gentle boil and you don't have any lumps from the flour.

Add the shredded cheddar cheese and keep on stirring! If you like thinner sauce, add the rest of the milk and stir it in completely. Turn the heat off, once the cheese is melted, and then add the cooked noodles to the sauce. Mix them well so that they are all covered in the sauce and enjoy!

Best Pizza Crust Ever

1 tablespoon yeast; 3 cups of flour; 2 tablespoons oil
½ teaspoon of sugar

1. In a small bowl, add 1 cup hot water with 1 tablespoon of yeast.
2. Now mix in 2 tablespoons of oil.

3. Mix all ingredients, in a large bowl, with a bread hook on an electric mixer or with your hands until the dough becomes a ball. If it is sticky, add a little more flour.
4. Cover with a towel and let it sit for an hour.
5. After the dough has risen, roll it out on a greased and floured pizza pan or cookie sheet.
6. Add your pizza sauce and some yummy, healthy toppings. Be creative and try something new!
7. Bake at a preheated oven at 425 for at least 13 minutes.

Great Salsa Dip

1 8 ounce package of softened cream cheese; 8-10 ounces of your favorite salsa; 1 tablespoon milk

In a blender, whip softened cream cheese until it is smooth. Add the milk during this process. Once cream cheese is silky smooth, begin adding your salsa. This step is really under your control because some people like their dip thinner than others. You can control how thick or thin your dip is during this step because you will add it a couple of ounces at a time.

Once your dip is made, put it in the fridge in a covered container for at least two hours so that it can harden up a bit and is cold when you serve it. Fill a platter with big chips and put your dip in a bowl in the center and invite a few friends over! Remember, no double dipping!

Scotcharoos

1 cup white corn syrup; 1 cup sugar
1 cup peanut butter; 6 cups Rice Krispies
1/2 bag chocolate chips; 1/2 bag butterscotch
chips

Boil syrup and sugar together. Remove from heat with first bubbles. Add peanut butter. Pour over cereal. Put in 13 x 9 pan. Melt chips together for frosting. Add a dab of peanut butter if you wish.

Basic Cooking Terms That Are Good to Know:

Bake -To cook something in an oven.
Boil -To cook food in a liquid so that the liquid gets hot enough to see bubbles; you can have a rapid boil on a high heat or a slow boil on a lower heat.
Chop -To cut into small pieces.
Drain -To remove all the liquid from something—usually using a strainer.
Grate or Shred -To scrape food against the holes of a grater. making thin pieces that sort of look like "scraps."
Grease -To lightly coat with oil or butter (or a non-stick spray) so food does not stick to the surface of the pan.
Marinate -To soak food in a liquid to tenderize or add flavor to it.
Mix -To stir ingredients together.
Preheat -To turn oven on ahead of time so that it is at the desired temperature for you to use it.

So, did cooking and all these numbers put you in the mood for more numbers? How about this brain teaser? How many addition signs should be put between digits of the number 987654321 and where should you put them to get a total of 99?

Strong Catholic Men of Today

You know guys, it's not like there are only great men from days gone by. The fact is, there are Catholic heroes today who are doing great things for the Kingdom of God, just like you can do now as a young man and then when you're a grown man that matters. These guys came from homes just like yours. Check it out.

Tom Monaghan

Thomas Steven Monaghan was born March 25, 1937 in Ann Arbor Michigan.

His father died when he was a child and his mother had difficulty raising him and his brother all by herself. He ended up in the St. Joseph Children's Home in Jackson, Michigan. The home was operated by the Felician Sisters and they inspired Tom to go to the minor seminary. However, Tom didn't make it to the priesthood because he was expelled for disciplinary reasons.

But the stage had been set for the ways in which God would be able to use Mr. Monaghan once he chose to be a soldier for Christ.

After that, Tom enlisted in the United States Marine Corps by mistake. He meant to join the army. Later, Tom was discharged honorably and returned to Michigan and started college at the University of Michigan.

He decided to study to become an architect. While he was a student, he and his brother borrowed money to buy a small pizza place called DomiNick's which grew into Domino's Pizza. Later on Tom bought out his brother with a car.

In 1983, Tom bought the Detroit Tigers and they won the World Series a year later. Over ten years later, he sold the team to the owner of Little Caesar's. During all of Tom's success he collected artifacts of the famous architect Frank Lloyd Wright. Monaghan purchased a portion of Drummond Island in Michigan for a private resort. He also had a passion for cars and had a nice collection. Tom enjoyed the best the world could offer.

After reading a book entitled *Mere Christianity* by C.S. Lewis, Tom realized he was living a life of pride. He took two years away from business to think about things of faith.

Thinking about his life, Tom gave up his wealthy lifestyle and started to help people. He built a new Cathedral in Nicaragua and a mission in Honduras. When he returned to his business the sales had fallen and he boosted them immediately. With his profit he supported pro life causes and made the pro abortion feminists super mad.

In 1998, Tom sold Domino's Pizza. He took that money and established the Mater Christi Foundation, today known as "the Ave Maria Foundation." Ave Maria is Latin and means "Hail Mary." That's what God's angel said, "Hail Mary," when he told Mary about her role in carrying the baby Jesus.

The Ave Maria Foundation focuses on Catholic education, media, community projects, and other Catholic charities. Ava Maria Radio is part of this enterprise.

He also established "the Ave Maria List," which is a pro life action committee. He wanted to help defend the rights of Christians so he set up the Thomas More Law Center that does just that. In countries of Central and South America the Ave Maria Foundation helps the poor.

Right in the beautiful city of Ann Arbor, Michigan, Tom helped to establish Spiritus Sanctus Academies, which are Catholic schools taught by the Dominican Sisters of Mary, Mother of the Eucharist. Recently, the foundation has focused on higher education. In 2000 the Ave Maria Law School opened in Ann Arbor, Michigan. The goal of the school is to educate good, moral attorneys who will make a difference in the world.

Tom Monaghan founded Ave Maria University and town in Florida in 2006. The plan is to build 11,000 homes and a church, with several businesses.

Not bad for one guy who started out at a children's home. The thing about working with God is that no matter what He calls you to do in your life, He will always be with you because He loves you so very much.

William Donohue

William Donohue was born July 18, 1947 in Manhattan, New York. He has made a name for himself by fighting discrimination against Catholics and the Church. He has gone after many public figures on television, radio, and print.

In the 1970s, Bill was teaching at St. Lucy's School in Harlem. He then changed his job and became a college professor at La Roche College in Pennsylvania. In 1980, he received a doctorate in Sociology from New York University.

While he was there in New York going to school, he became the director of the Catholic League. The organization was founded to counteract Anti-Catholicism in the American culture.

It may not always be easy to be Catholic but it is always right.

Since Mr. Donohue has taken charge of the Catholic League, he has been very vocal about protecting the Catholic Church. The organization publishes a magazine called The Catalyst, which lets the readers know who, how, and when the Catholic faith is being insulted.

God's graces abound for you because He loves you!

By making people aware of what is said about the Church, Bill has been able to get some folks to stop badmouthing Catholic teaching and traditions. Mr. Donohue is a true warrior for Jesus.

Fr. Frank Pavone

Frank Anthony Pavone was born February 4, 1959 in Port Chester, New York. His father was a shoe maker supplier. Frank grew up close to Church and attended regularly. He was a server and enjoyed school. Young Frank was a very intelligent boy and graduated valedictorian of his class. During his sophomore year, he began attending daily Mass. By the time he graduated he had heard his call from God: the priesthood! When he told his pastor, this kind priest replied, "I have been praying for that!"

Frank attended the Don Bosco College and Seminary in New Jersey. He attended the March for Life in Washington D.C. during his college years. This began his interest in the pro life movement. In 1981, he graduated again valedictorian with a Philosophy degree and a teacher's certification in Math, English and Classical Languages. Frank made his temporary vows and became a Salesian brother, continuing his studies to become a priest.

During this time, Pavone worked with youth at summer camps. Finally, on November 12, 1988, he was ordained a priest. He began his priesthood at a parish in Staten Island.

Here, Fr. Pavone expanded three important areas of the parish:

✝ the Archdiocesan Deaconate program
✝ evangelization through cable television
✝ pro-life awareness

Father was a really busy guy! Soon, his work went beyond New York to the entire nation because Fr. Pavone became the leader of Priests for Life.

Fr. Pavone serves on many pro life boards all over the country and works tirelessly to bring the message of life to all people. He has helped to promote life by making public the stories of people such as Gianna Jessen, an abortion survivor and the Schindler family. The Schindlers were forced to allow and watch their disabled daughter Terri Schiavo starve to death.

This was a tragic situation where Terri's husband no longer wanted to be bothered with her and wouldn't allow her family to care for her. Instead Terri's husband wanted her gone, dead. Fr. Pavone became the family's spiritual director and also the spokesperson for them.

With his God-given intellect and gifts, Father Pavone tries to make this world better through his pro life work.

How do these men, and the men in your life that you admire, stack up against who the world "worships?"

Remember that success to God is often very different than success according to the world... and you should live your life being a success for God!

Y	U	I	O	D	P	Q	W	E	B	E	R	T	Y
P	Q	W	E	R	D	I	G	N	I	T	Y	T	Y
U	A	I	O	P	A	S	D	C	B	F	L	G	M
H	J	T	K	L	C	V	B	O	L	N	I	M	I
P	O	I	R	H	U	Y	T	U	E	R	F	E	G
A	S	D	F	I	M	V	I	R	T	U	E	V	U
D	K	F	G	V	O	H	J	A	K	L	M	N	E
Z	I	X	C	A	N	T	D	G	B	V	N	M	L
E	N	R	Q	L	A	T	I	E	Y	O	U	I	P
J	O	P	A	R	G	S	S	S	D	C	F	G	R
H	O	J	K	Y	H	L	C	M	M	A	R	Y	O
Z	M	S	N	X	A	V	E	A	U	T	I	T	R
S	W	J	E	K	N	L	R	M	M	I	T	G	H
I	E	R	D	P	V	D	N	E	K	O	L	W	K
O	I	U	Y	T	H	O	R	M	O	N	E	S	R
J	E	S	U	S	L	O	V	E	S	Y	O	U	✝

1. Everybody's got it.
2. The ability to confront fear or uncertainty.
3. Good habits.
4. Love and devotion to country.
5. Basic instructions before leaving earth.
6. The real deal.
7. Queen of Heaven.
8. He relied on disguises so he could serve others.
9. A call from God.
10. To pray and ask God.
11. The code a knight lives by.
12. Patron Saint of the Universal Catholic Church.
13. Chemicals in the body.
14. Largest organ of the body.
15. Established the Ave Maria Foundation.

Basic
Combat
Training

Your Battles...

You know that in order to win a war, soldiers have to train. Obviously, battles are not won by chance. Basic combat training transforms boys into men and men into real soldiers. Their training includes, among other things, fitness, nutrition, and learning to work as a team. The goal of this training is to become great soldiers, able to defend their country by winning the war.

In order to win the battle for Heaven, you need to have a plan of training as well. Here is a simple but effective plan you can use your entire life to complete your training here and attain your heavenly goal.

Morning Offering

It'll be tough to win the war if you lose your first battle. It is sometimes difficult to get up and out of bed on a school day morning. This, then, is your first battle of the day. The sheets seem to be glued to your body! The warm bed doesn't want to let go of you! It requires courage to wake up and face the day. This is especially true if you've been facing a bully or have problems with a particular subject.

To get off to a good start, it's a great idea to say the morning offering, which is a prayer to say "hi!" to Jesus and entrust yourself to Him. Kneel down next to your bed and tell Jesus how hard it is to get up and get ready for school; tell Him you'll live this day for Him, to give

Him glory. You can make up your own special prayer, or you can choose one to memorize.

For example, here is a very simple prayer:

"Good morning Jesus, I give you this day, all that I think, and do and say; I will work, have fun; laugh and play; Jesus be with me, all through the day, Amen."

Or...

"O Jesus, through the Immaculate Heart of Mary, I offer You my prayers, works, joys and sufferings of this day for all the intentions of Your Sacred Heart, in union with the Holy Sacrifice of the Mass throughout the world, in reparation for my sins, for the intentions of all my relatives and friends, and in particular for the intentions of the Holy Father. Amen."

You have won the first battle, and it is an important one!

Daily Prayer

Prayer is talking to Jesus. It is amazing! Remember that Jesus prayed and openly encouraged his disciples to pray. And guess what, you are also His disciple! So, how does a person learn to pray?

Start by setting aside five minutes of your day to sit down in a quiet place where there are no distractions— not in front of the computer! Place yourself in the presence of Jesus, asking your guardian angel to help you start a conversation with Jesus. You can talk to Him as you talk to your best friend! Tell Him the things that are concerning you, what is making you happy, angry or sad; God is always listening.

You may say something like: "Hi Jesus, today I had a hard time at school. I forgot to hand in my homework. I'm so mad at myself 'cause I spent so much time working on it.... Tonight mom is driving me to practice, it'll be fun. Help me to play good and be good sport with the rest of the team..." On you go, you are praying!

Daily prayer is like the fuel that keeps the engine moving; give it a try!

The Holy Rosary

On a cold winter day, the police chief and his team of men were at the subway station. A newspaper reporter was there to be the first one to take pictures and write an article about this event. He approached the police chief, who seemed to be whispering something, to ask him a few questions. The police chief told the reporter that they were waiting for the next train to arrive to arrest a criminal.

The reporter noticed that he had his right hand in his pocket, when the police chief asked him: "Do you want to see my weapon?" "Oh, sure sir," answered the reporter. The police chief took his hand out of his pocket, and he was holding a Rosary. "Here, Son, this is my weapon."

Yes, praying the Holy Rosary is one of the most powerful weapons! Our Lady listens to all her children's requests. When you pray the rosary you contemplate Moments in the lives of Jesus and Mary on each mystery. The rosary is divided into four parts: each part into five mysteries. For each mystery one Our Father and Ten Hail Mary's are prayed while you meditate on a certain time of Jesus' life.

The name rosary means "crown of roses." Think about each of the Hail Mary's you pray as a rose offered to Our Lady. By the end of the rosary, you have offered her a huge bouquet of roses! If saying the entire rosary seems like a big task, start out with just one decade and slowly add one at a time. The idea is to make the effort and to keep on trying. Never forget that praying the Rosary is your most powerful weapon!

Examination of Conscience at Night

At the end of the day, a soldier needs to evaluate how his training went that day. Did he make any progress? Before going to bed, it's a good idea to take a quick look at your day in God's presence to see if you have behaved as a soldier of Christ, a true son of God. An easy way to do this is by asking yourself these three questions:

✠ What did I do today that was pleasing to God?
✠ What did I do today that was not pleasing to God?
✠ What does God want me to do better tomorrow?

Ponder briefly on each question, and then follow with an act of contrition to tell Jesus that you are sorry for having offended Him.

An Act of Contrition is just a short prayer telling Jesus you are sorry for your sins. It can be as simple as, "I'm sorry, Lord. Help me do better tomorrow."

Or, it can be the traditional act of contrition:

Oh my God, I am heartily sorry for having offended thee and I detest all my sins because of the loss of Heaven and the pains of Hell, But most of all because they offend Thee my God who are all good and deserving of all my love. I firmly resolve with the help of Thy grace, to confess my sins, to do penance and to amend my life, Amen.

Pray three Hail Mary's at night before going to bed asking the Blessed Mother to help you keep your heart pure.

Confession

Going to confession has gotten a bad rap lately. Some people may say, "that's an old fashioned thing," or "I don't need to go to confession, I haven't killed anybody." They are so wrong! Confession is an awesome Sacrament where not only your sins are forgiven, but you are also able to receive the graces you need to grow in holiness. Besides, the things that we sometimes feel are no big deal are really a big deal to God—so going to confession, with a truly sorry heart for what you've done and a sincere interest in not doing it again is a gift God gives YOU! It is your chance to wipe the slate clean, so to speak. Isn't that a great gift?

Let's look at this a bit more. Sin is saying "NO" to God. It's telling God: "I'm going to do it my way, and not Your way." All humans have a tendency to sin, some more than others. When a soldier is sent to combat, he takes along his weapon. Along with the rosary, going to confession frequently is your weapon against sin.

The Catholic Church teaches that there are two kinds of sins: mortal and venial. When a person commits a mortal sin, he or she is totally dead to the life of God in his or her soul. It's like

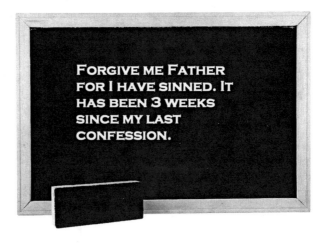

FORGIVE ME FATHER FOR I HAVE SINNED. IT HAS BEEN 3 WEEKS SINCE MY LAST CONFESSION.

cutting all communication with God. Confession restores that communication: fills you up with God's grace to begin again. God is so merciful, He will always forgive you if you are truly sorry, no matter how grave your sins. That's because His love for you is so immense that He wants you to spend eternity in Heaven with Him.

Venial sins do not cut you completely off from God, but do "stain" your soul and your relationship with God. That's why you need to do your best to avoid them.

Always remember that your priest is your friend. He is working for God and will help you get to Heaven. If you aren't sure if what you've done is wrong, or what kind of sin it may be, talk to your priest. Don't ever be afraid of him. And every single thing you say to him is a secret. He is bound by his vows to never repeat what is said in a confession, so don't wait any longer. Accept this great gift of God's and get to confession on a regular basis.

**Don't delay,
Start your basic combat training today!**

Basic Combat Training: Make a chart like this one to help you keep track of your progress.

Day	Morning offering	Daily prayer	Holy Rosary	3 Hail Mary's	Examination of Conscience
1					
2					
3					
4					
5					
6					
7					
8					
9					
10					
11					
12					
13					
14					
15					
16					
17					
and so on					

Game Systems versus the Catholic Church

Do you own a game system? Is it a PS3? Maybe it's the older PS2. Or is it an Xbox? Maybe you have an older brother or sister and they have a Nintendo.

Hey, do you want a laugh? Ask your Dad what game system he played on and you might find out it is something as ancient as a Sega or Atari. Or you may just find out that he didn't have a game system.

Poor guy.

What's the Point?

The point is simple, you live in a world where what is cool today will be totally different tomorrow. The "Must-Have" game system you or your friends are dying to have will be totally outdated in a year or two. This is a fact, just look at a timeline of all the game systems for the past dozen years.

Another fact is that your Catholic faith doesn't change. That's a fact you can count on! What was true yesterday is still true today and will be true tomorrow.

God doesn't change so the Truth shouldn't change. Faith isn't like a game system whose popularity comes and goes. Faith is what you should build your life upon. Faith gives you Truths that have withstood the test of time. Your Catholic faith is  thousands of years old. Imagine a game system lasting that long. It ain't gonna happen. The only thing that will hold up over time is the Catholic Faith because it is the Truth.

Is there a second point?

You bet there is, and it isn't that God doesn't want you to have fun, because He does. It's just that you also have to be making good decisions about how you spend your time. Since you know that things like game systems come and go but your faith is here to stay, you need to give your faith some of your time. Maybe it doesn't seem like it now, but time with God—in other words, prayer—helps make your life better.

If you are addicted to a game system that is going to be outdated in a year or two (that's a fact) and God will never be outdated, why not give God more of your gaming time?

Your faith is an amazing gift so…

learn it, love it, live it!

Becoming a man that matters is all about making the right choices.

It is really all about questions and answers and knowledge:

☦ Take time to know God and His love for you.
☦ Always remember that you are created in the image of God and that is what gives you great dignity.
☦ God does have a plan for you—a vocation. Answer His call to find true happiness in life.
☦ Pope Benedict XVI says that kids ought to use the Internet and the media to evangelize. *This means you control it and it doesn't control you!*
☦ In order to win the "battle" for Heaven, you need a plan—start it today!

1-c; 2-a; 3-g; 4-h; 5-b; 6-f; 7-e; 8-d

Brain teasers on page 100:

1. **your breath**
2. **the word "Wholesome"**

Word Search

				D				B					
P				D	I	G	N	I	T	Y			
	A						C	B			L		M
		T		C			O	L			I		I
			R	H			U	E			F		G
	S			I	M	V	I	R	T	U	E		U
	K			V	O			A			V		E
	I			A	N	T	D	G			O		L
	N			L	A		I	E			C		P
J				R	G		S	S			C		R
	O			Y	H		C		M	A	R	Y	O
		S		A			C	E			T		
			E	N			R				I		
			P				N				O		
				H	O	R	M	O	N	E	S		
J	E	S	U	S	L	O	V	E	S	Y	O	U	✝

Brain teaser on page 138:

9+8+7+65+4+3+2+1 = 99 would be 7 addition signs OR
9+8+7+6+5+43+21 = 99 would be 6 addition signs

Notes to self. Optional but worthwhile...

Consider some of the things you read and decide how they will make a difference in your life.

_____
_____
_____
_____
_____
_____
_____
_____
_____
_____

Who did you find most inspiring? Father Pro or maybe Mr. Donohue? What about that St. Joseph? Amazing men, right?

_____
_____
_____
_____
_____
_____
_____
_____
_____
_____

CPSIA information can be obtained at www.ICGtesting.com
Printed in the USA
268010BV00004B/1/P